Shadows Point to Rainbows

*An Unwanted Dog Becomes
an Injured Boy's Best Friend*

Linda Franklin

TEACH Services, Inc.
P U B L I S H I N G
www.TEACHServices.com • (800) 367-1844

World rights reserved. This book or any portion thereof may not be copied or reproduced in any form or manner whatever, except as provided by law, without the written permission of the publisher, except by a reviewer who may quote brief passages in a review.

The author assumes full responsibility for the accuracy of all facts and quotations as cited in this book. The opinions expressed in this book are the author's personal views and interpretations, and do not necessarily reflect those of the publisher.

This book is provided with the understanding that the publisher is not engaged in giving spiritual, legal, medical, or other professional advice. If authoritative advice is needed, the reader should seek the counsel of a competent professional.

Copyright © 2020 Linda Franklin
Copyright © 2020 TEACH Services, Inc.
ISBN-13: 978-1-4796-1126-3 (Paperback)
ISBN-13: 978-1-4796-1127-0 (ePub)
Library of Congress Control Number: 2020901704

Edited by Linda Marie Steinke Harrington and TEACH Services, Inc.

Unless otherwise indicated, all Scripture is from the King James Version.

Published by

www.TEACHServices.com • (800) 367-1844

Dedication

This book is dedicated to my granddaughter
Hannah May Franklin
*a young lady with a beautiful heart who has inherited
an insatiable appetite for inspiring stories.*

Dear Hannah,

When I travel beside you in the car, or when we sit together down at the river, you almost never fail to ask me for a story. You don't want to hear just *any* story—you want to hear about the times God protected me in my childhood. I take my responsibility seriously. Fathers and mothers, grandmas and grandpas are admonished to repeat their stories of God's protection down through the generations.

> Make sure you don't forget the things your eyes have seen
> and your ears have heard.
> Don't let them slip from your hearts
> or you'll lose your love for the Lord and your appreciation
> of what He has done for you.
> Teach these things to your children and grandchildren
> and share your experiences with them so they,
> too, will love the Lord.
> (Deuteronomy 4:9, *The Clear Word*)

This book is a collection of faith-building events that happened to your father when he was chosen by a very special dog that helped him watch for rainbows. "Champion" helped him discover how shadows sharpen our focus. Clouds will eventually part if we watch carefully for that special place where rainbows are born. That's faith, Hannah—the ability to trust that a shadow has as great a purpose as the rainbow—they both indicate the source of light behind us.

Your experience is your history—"His story" in you. There will never be a threat on the horizon ahead that you and your Best Friend can't handle together. Don't be surprised when I start asking *you* for a story!

Love,
Grandma

Table of Contents

Introduction . . . . *vii*

Chapter 1: The Visitor 9
Opportunity knocked, courage answered.

Chapter 2: Enchanting Walk 21
A walk in the sunshine reveals a surprising secret.

Chapter 3: The Incredible Gift 29
Do not fear to hope, even when hoping seems hopeless.

Chapter 4: Unexpected Advice 43
When there's no other way, God touches hearts.

Chapter 5: Learning Obedience 53
Gentle repetition is the key to learning obedience.

Chapter 6: Hard Work 67
Rest if you must, but never say quit!

Chapter 7: The Last Trick 79
The most important lesson is learned in the last mile.

Chapter 8: True Blue 91
Just showing up is half the stress of the victor's cup!

Chapter 9: "Please Don't Die!" 103
The desperate plea of a little boy is heard.

Chapter 10: Happy Trails 117
Enjoyable memories don't just happen; we must create them.

Chapter 11: Due North 135
As the needle to the pole, a true friend points upward.

Chapter 12: All Growed Up 147
Gentleman's farewell; the crowning act of a true champion.

Chapter 13: Encircled 159
"O that everyone might be this happy!" —Jed Franklin, 2017

Chapter 14: Living Under the Rainbow 167
Sharing Survival Skills.

Gems from Jed *175*

Bibliography *179*

Introduction

I shudder to think of how close I came to turning a deaf ear to Champion's plea for help at a time when he desperately needed a home. Though I have never seen an angel, the night I adopted Champ floats to the top of my list of divine encounters. Could I have known what a powerful impact that dear dog would have on my son's survival, I would have gladly waited all night to take him home.

After my son's accident, Champion was Jed's joy-support system. There is no doubt at all in my mind that Champ helped Jed carry, without shame, the scars that have held many burn survivors socially immobilized for life. Looking back over the years, I am ever so grateful for the qualities of adaptability and perseverance, among other spiritual strengths, that Jed learned from Champ. It thrills my soul to see Jed handing down these same character traits to the next generation of Franklins, my grandchildren.

Champion was a strong force for good; he did not ignore shadows; he let them direct his destiny. He's the only dog I ever knew who could see a rainbow.

> Silence in the soul makes more distinct the voice of God.
> (Ellen G. White, *Our Father Cares*, p. 162)

Chapter 1

The Visitor

Opportunity knocked, courage answered.

I am his friend, and for that cause I walk
Not overclose beside him, leaving still
Space for his silences, and space for mine.
—Barbara Young, in "I Hear it Said"

Tramp

Jed is dawdling over his breakfast. There is no sunshine in his corner of the world. The spruce trees around the little trailer park we temporarily call "home" in southwest Washington are nearly invisible in the foggy mist. His favorite person in the whole world, his father, Jere, has just left for work. Jed pushes a forkful of pancake across his plate; white paths emerge in the peach sauce behind his excavation. Loader-style—with square and slow, robotic movements—he lifts a bite to his mouth. He is not eating as much as he is waiting and hoping—seeking to sweep a little brightness toward himself. He's an outdoors boy. What does he have to look forward to but washing the breakfast dishes and doing homeschool with Mom?

Awaiting the dissolving of the indoor gloom that seems to have settled over the breakfast table, I decide to mix up a batch of bread. I know that Jed's inventive mind will enable him to dispel the shadows that have hounded our tracks for the past three years of our sojourn from Canada.

Jed's fork brakes hard on a hairpin curve at the edge of his plate. As he lifts the bite in preparation for the straight-line entry to the tunnel of his mouth, there comes a tapping at the kitchen door. Our eyes meet under surprised brows. We hardly know anyone here in Brush Prairie. So, who could it be? I cover my dough with the mixing bowl and quickly wash my hands.

"Expecting company?"

My eight-year-old shakes his head and then brightens, quickly dropping his loaded fork and nearly overturning his chair in his haste to reach the door.

> *Envisioning a ragged, shoeless beggar on our porch, I see tomorrow's news headline flash into view: "Homeless Stranger Attacks Mother and Son."*

"Tramp!" Jed grins around the treasured word. "He's here! I told him to come back, but ..."

"A tramp?" I grab Jed's arm with a wet hand. "A homeless man?"

"He's a friend I stuck up for yesterday when the neighbor boys were shooting at him," Jed says, straining against my grip.

"Shooting? Right here in Brush Prairie, Washington?"

Jed knows I detest weapons of any kind. I cup my son's chin in my hand and steer his head so that I can look into his eyes.

He turns my way and says, "Aw Mommy, it was just some boys in the trailer court showing off their BB guns. But they *could* have hurt him. In fact, they *meant* to! They said, 'He's bad. He doesn't *b'long* here.' I stood in front of him and told 'em, 'He's with me!' So, they told me to leave. He came with me yesterday."

Envisioning a ragged, shoeless beggar on our porch, I see tomorrow's news headline flash into view: "Homeless Stranger Attacks Mother and Son." Then, in another flash, an inner Voice softens the jagged edge of fear—*"Inasmuch as ye have done it unto one of the least of these ..."*

"C'mon, Mommy!" Jed says, dragging me toward an uncertain future.

"Think he's been watching our house all morning since Daddy left?" I whisper.

Jed frowns, then, tossing me a broad grin, he throws open the door. My jaw drops. I quickly inhale. There sits a beautiful German shepherd, wagging his tail as if to ask, "Can my new friend come out and play?"

"Can this 'Tramp' come in, Mommy?" Jed says with a twinkle in his eye—not just for the visitor but also for so successfully involving me in his mystery.

Jed has a habit of dispersing clouds with spontaneous outbursts of sunshine … or maybe even flashes of lightning. I drop my hand from my mouth and shake the paw that the dog offers. His quick inspection of our trailer house reveals two perfectly good, unclaimed pancakes at the edge of the table.

"Doesn't he remind you of our Tramp, Mommy?" Jed asked, tearing one pancake in half and smearing it unevenly with peanut butter. "Look! He even likes PB!"

The Road of Life

It's true—this new dog has Tramp's identical coloring and markings—brindle with a dab of white on the last few tail hairs. He is obviously at ease with us. My heart for a dog has been on hold for well over a year since Tramp's death. But, under the gaze of these golden eyes, that cold place in my heart is getting warmer. We leave the breakfast dishes soaking, the bread rising, and head toward the living room for our reading time.

"Why don't the other boys like this dog, Jed? Is he dangerous? Why doesn't he have a collar? Has he had his shots?"

None of these mother worries bothered Jed. He wouldn't care if his new friend had rabies. Just like our old Tramp, the dog lay comfortably at our feet with his eyes on Jed, as if ready to listen as we revisited Jed's favorite allegory, *Hinds' Feet on High Places*. As the chapter we are reading, "Invitation to the High Places," comes to an end, the sun peeks shyly through the clouds.

"It's so much easier for me to see mistakes in Much Afraid's journey than my own. Why is that, Mom?"

"You will be able to see that clearly as you grow up, Jed. Your life is a book. Each day is a new page. You are the writer. Your story is unfolding day by day. God chooses the beginning and the setting as well as some of the characters in your book, but it is you who ultimately chooses how it will end. There are only two options. Life is a journey."

Jed nods his head slowly, as, once again, he grasps the metaphor of life's journey that Jere and I have shared with him more than once in his short life span. Then, our country boy glances up at the sunshine calling him outside.

"Gotta make play while the sun shines, Mom!"

"Repeat your memory verse, first, please."

"Let not your heart be troubled. Ye believe in God, believe also in me. In my Father's house are many mansions: if it were not so I would have told you. I go to prepare a place for you. And if I go and prepare a place for you, I will come again, and receive you unto myself; that where I am there ye may be also."

"Good job!" I said, patting Jed with one hand and his new friend with the other. "We'll postpone the remainder of your homeschool lessons for a couple of hours while I finish lettering those posters for Dad and get the bread baked. If the weather holds, we might try tackling your spelling words outside today, but, listen to me now! If those boys show up with their guns, you two come right back inside!"

"No problem!" Jed says, grabbing his jacket. "They're at school."

I can see Jed and the dog from the kitchen window as I shape my dough into loaves. He steers his large, metal Tonka truck onto the edge of the driveway, leaving a tire imprint in the fresh mud. After a few minutes of roadmaking, my boy and "his" dog head toward a small clump of saplings near the edge of our yard, which Jed calls his "wilderness." The only thing he loves more than making roads is a peaceful hour in the woods discovering worms, spiders, insects, and other treasures he can tell us about.

Happy is the lad who experiences close kinship with trees and dogs and makes the most of mud. Jed is our rainbow over the muddy road of life, preventing us from dwelling in the shadows. I know, in my head, that all things do work together for good, but these last couple of years have been especially hard on my heart. Might this new dog become part of our saga?

Is it fair to allow Jed to hope—to love this dog—only to endure the pain of separation when our road forks again? A fork in the road can be the knife that cuts us a spoonful of memories. How we choose to remember the past is a reflection of our character—whether we take it as a random collection of unrelated happenings or as an orchestrated series of events. Our witness is our legacy. I would like to be able to wash off the mud and tell my story without antagonists, but that would be no story at all. There must be an interaction and a problem to overcome, a defeat followed by a victory.

Mystery Dog

The smell of fresh bread awakens me from my daydream as I finish lettering the last poster for the upcoming cooking school to be held at the restaurant where Jed's father is the Director of Public Relations. I peek into the refrigerator. Today we have a treat—a tasty leftover entrée from the restaurant, a layered burrito casserole. Jed's father is hoping to find employment in his specialty field of microbiology, but, in the meantime, we're thankful for the restaurant work, a community outreach for healthy living.

From the kitchen window I can see that Pat, the manager of our suburban trailer court, is out for her morning walk. I step outside to greet her. The air is warm and friendly—like Pat's smile. Pointing to the dog, I ask if she knows anything about our new "Tramp."

"I think he lives down the r-r-road a mile or two, Linda," she says, trilling her "r" with a bit of an Irish brogue, pointing out of the court drive to the left. "Seems like a nice enough animal most of the time but does that dag ivver-r-r hate guns! My boys like to shoot at bir-r-rds and squir-r-rels after school and that dag allus gr-r-rowls at 'em! M'boys are afr-r-raid of him and don't want him ar-r-round. I've hear-r-rd 'em call 'im Champ when they'r-r-re chasin' 'im away."

As Pat leaves, I sit in the sunshine on the front porch, savoring the rich aroma of familiar country scents—damp leaves, overturned topsoil, and fresh-baked bread.

Champ ... Champion—a good name. Such a beautiful shepherd. I wonder though—can he be trusted? Shepherds can be very protective.

With an involuntary shudder, I recall the vivid details of an incident that took place when I was in the third grade. It convinced me not to trespass into a German shepherd's yard. As if to ease my worried thoughts, Champ raises his head, looks in my direction, and wags his tail. I smile and nod. Everything is OK. I close my eyes; I hear a single engine plane droning overhead, a robin singing, bees humming nearby, and Jed talking to Champion. I open my eyes. Champion is listening, with ears erect and tail wagging at appropriate intervals.

> A boy and his dog make a glorious pair:
> No better friendship is found anywhere,
> For they talk and they walk and they run and they play,
> And they have their deep secrets for many a day;
> And that boy has a comrade who thinks and who feels,
> Who walks down the road with a dog at his heels.
>
> He may go where he will and his dog will be there,
> May revel in mud and his dog will not care;
> Faithful he'll stay for the slightest command
> And bark with delight at the touch of his hand;
> Oh, he owns a treasure which nobody steals,
> Who walks down the road with a dog at his heels.

> No other can lure him away from his side;
> He's proof against riches and station and pride;
> Fine dress does not charm him, and flattery's breath
> Is lost on the dog, for he's faithful to death;
> He sees the great soul which the body conceals—
> Oh, it's great to be young with a dog at your heels!
> —Edgar A. Guest, "A Boy and His Dog"

A Pattern Emerges

Later that week, Champion again taps on the door just as Jed finishes his school lessons for the day. That afternoon they explore the fields surrounding our trailer park, dig holes in the soft earth seeking buried treasure, watch nests, and build roads. Lying side by side in the grass, they quietly watch the clouds. There is no need of words when a boy loves his dog. Champion is a real gift for Jed. Where did he come from? Where does he belong? He looks well cared for, but ...

Someday I must find out who Champion belongs to. He's just the dog Jed needs—intelligent, mannerly, good-natured, and loyal. I think I might be able to make room in my heart for this very intelligent animal, but he belongs to someone else, and he looks valuable. Are we just supposed to enjoy him while we can? If only this arrangement was permanent ... but I don't know if Jere's heart is open yet.

Whenever Champion comes in the morning, he spends the whole day with Jed, but if he does not appear until after lunch, he only comes for an hour or two and leaves at about 6 pm as if he knows he must be home before dark.

Just about the time we've accustomed ourselves to saying "Champ" instead of "Tramp," and think we have his schedule figured out, he quits coming—altogether. Two long weeks pass without his familiar tap at the kitchen door. Jed never loses hope.

"You miss your Tennessee friends, Michael and Daniel?" I ask Jed during Champ's absence. Jed had made good friends with two boys in our apartment complex near Takoma Hospital in Greenville, Tennessee, when Jere was lab director for a year.

Jed and his friends from our apartment complex had a backyard "camping trip." Jed came back with a broken camping candle that he'd been saving for the event.

"What happened to your candle?" I asked.

"It broke."

"How'd it get broken?"

"I was testing it—to see how strong it was."

"Oh, I see," I nodded. "How strong was it?"

"Not very."

Jed was optimistic enough to appreciate the past and not anticipate future shadows.

He and his friends had some interesting times playing with snapping turtles and snakes while I kept hoping there would be no poisonous encounters. "Yeah, I do miss them, Mommy," Jed replies with downcast eyes, "but a visit from Champ will be nice!" Jed was optimistic enough to appreciate the past and not anticipate future shadows.

Butterscotch

Jed has always loved orange cats. Back when he was six years of age, he decided to pray for one. I doubted this prayer would be answered because Jere and I did not share Jed's enthusiasm for cats of any color because we love feeding and watching birds. But one never knows how Providence will view a child's prayer. My doubts were no disservice to Jed's faith, however. The very next day, an orange cat came out of the forest and walked right up to Jed who was making roads in the dust at our temporary very country location in the Blue Mountains of north central Oregon. Within an hour after meeting "Peaches," he was holding the gifts she bestowed on him—her six kittens—each one as brilliantly orange as she was!

Now, during Champ's absence, another orange cat appears in the driveway. She's a soft pastel ginger color, not quite fully grown, and she seems to have some kind of internal injury. Jed names her "Butterscotch" and cares for her with total devotion for two days, while she purrs in appreciation. Despite Jed's prayers, however, little Butterscotch does not survive. How will he handle the loss?

Having been in the neighborhood only a few weeks, Jed is the newcomer on the block, but that doesn't prevent him from organizing a funeral for his furry friend that afternoon, a celebration that involves several neighborhood children—including the boys who'd been shooting at Champion the day Jed came to his rescue. Casey brings a shovel. Another boy supplies a shoebox. Someone else offers a piece of cloth in which to wrap the body of the deceased. For about an hour, the children take turns digging a hole in the rocky soil of the back yard while Jed fashions a grave marker from a rough two-by-six with a black felt pen. When Jed decides that the hole is deep enough, he gently wraps his friend's limp body in the cloth, places it in the shoebox, and reverently lays it in the shallow grave.

The boys remove their baseball caps and bow their heads, imitating grown-up grief. I try to listen to Jed's prayer from an inconspicuous position in the back yard, but I can't quite hear it. After the prayer, the boys take turns throwing handfuls of dirt into the shallow grave. To finish the ceremony, Jed pounds the marker into position.

After the children have gone, I inspect the "headstone." On the board, Jed has drawn a smiley face, with its smile upside-down and teardrops falling.

After the funeral, Jed asks, "Mommy, where do animals go when they die?" He was trying not to cry, but his chin was quivering.

"I asked my mother the same question when I was about your age, Jed. Like you, I collected discarded animals—birds, rats, mice, and fish. School friends brought me their sick and damaged pets. I could not ignore my burning desire to do what I could to help them, but they often died. The thrill of the rescue outweighed the risk of death. When my pets died,

Mamma used to sing to me about a dog named 'Shep.' The song never failed to make me cry, but the last line was comforting: *'But if dogs have a heaven, there's one thing I know, Old Shep has a wonderful home.'*

"Animals are important to God. According to the Bible, God created animals before He breathed life into Adam. The eleventh chapter of Isaiah states that there will be animals in the new earth. God uses animals to teach us lessons about unconditional love. It would be in keeping with God's loving-kindness to re-create and return our pets to us when He forms the new earth, but I am willing to leave that decision in His hands. What I do know is that: first, God gave animals for us to love, and, second, love and pain go together. Should we stop loving because it hurts?"

Jed shakes his head and wipes a dusty arm across his moist cheek leaving a dark smudge that reminds me of the stain that sin has left upon humankind.

"Death is a big subject, Jed. It was not God's original plan that anything should die. Death hurts. It's not easy to understand or accept. Maybe we can read more about it in the Bible tonight, OK?"

Jed nods, takes the disposable cup filled with water that I offer him, and goes outside to pick some wildflowers for the new grave.

The Returning Champion

Two weeks after his departure, Champion returns. At the much-anticipated tap, both Jed and I hurry to the kitchen door. Champ slowly limps in and lays down, belly up, as if to explain the reason for his absence. Freshly healed, pink scars accompany large purple bruises covering his tummy and one hind leg. Apparently, he has had an accident, most likely with a vehicle on the road. I wonder if he was hurt on his way to visit Jed that nearly fateful day.

One day in late July, when Champion again misses a visit, Jed loses heart for his usual activities, especially school. What's a mother to do? Bribe, coddle, or sing maybe? I send up a plea for help while I finish folding clothes. Pondering the best use of time on this beautiful but very busy day, the sunshine reminds me of a quote that has been fluttering around like a butterfly in my mind.

> The most exalted spiritual truths may be brought home
> to the heart by the things of nature. The birds of the air,
> the flowers of the field in their glowing beauty,
> the springing grain, the fruitful branches of the vine,
> the trees putting forth their tender buds, the glorious sunset,
> the crimson clouds predicting a fair morrow,
> the recurring seasons—
> all these may teach us precious lessons of trust and faith.
> (Ellen G. White, *Counsels on Health*, p. 202)

Bobbing unsteadily like a wren caught in a cross wind on a thin branch, an idea hovers in my heart, attempting to land on the proverbial green bough abiding there. Would I assist its safe landing or ignore it and go on with my work while Jed struggles? He is not applying himself to what should be a short and simple assignment, and I have reminded him about his lack of dedication more than once in the last hour. His heart is outside in the sunshine. With heavy tread, another quotation marches through my mind.

> Smile, parents; smile, teachers.
> If your heart is sad, let not your face reveal the fact.
> Let the sunshine from a loving, grateful heart light up the countenance.
> Unbend from your iron dignity, adapt yourselves to the children's needs, and make them love you. You must win their affection,
> if you would impress religious truth upon their heart.
> (Ellen G. White, *The Adventist Home*, p. 432)

Yes, it felt like it was time for me to suggest a walk. As it turns out, it was the beginning of an extremely significant journey.

Chapter 2

Enchanting Walk

A walk in the sunshine reveals a surprising secret.

> It's how do you live and neighbor,
> How do you work and play,
> It's how do you say "good morning"
> To the people along the way,
> And it's how do you face your troubles
> Whenever your skies are gray.
> —Edgar A. Guest in "What Counts"

Timely Journey

Never one to question my motivation for taking a walk, Jed nods enthusiastically and accomplishes with passion, what could never have happened in his doldrums. While I fix lunch, Jed efficiently finishes his assignments, puts his schoolbooks away, tidies his room, and sits down to his favorite summertime lunch—fresh corn on the cob and tomato sandwiches with a thick slab of Walla Walla Sweet onion. We're soon on our way.

Like a bright rainbow-colored serving of fruit sorbet for dessert, the lanes, driveways, pathways, and gardens of our hobby-farm community are fairly exploding with brilliant colors of every shade: there are purple pansies and clover blossoms; magenta fuchsias; blue delphinium, jays, and forget-me-nots; unlimited shades of green; yellow marigolds and goldfinches; bright orange poppies and zinnias; and a gorgeous carpet of deep red petunias in front of a white farmhouse. No day has ever been more perfect for a walk.

> We should devote time to interest our children.
> We can walk out with them in the open air.
> A change will have a happy influence upon them.
> We can sit with them in the groves, and in the bright sunshine,
> and give their restless minds something to feed upon
> by conversing with them upon the works of God,
> and inspire them with love and reverence by calling
> their attention to the beautiful objects in nature.
> (Ellen G. White, *Review and Herald*, May 30, 1871, Art. B)

Side by side in a field of daisies, we savor a handful of wild blackberries as we study the cumulus clouds forming animal shapes against the bright blue sky. My ears are tuned to the northwest Oregon sounds I grew up with under the shadow of Mt. Hood: the distant drone of a chain saw and the rhythmic "bump-bumpety-bump" of a square baler preserving a field of alfalfa for the coming winter.

When our berries are gone, Jed makes his most common request, "Tell me a story, Mom."

"Hmm. Let me think, Jed," I respond, loath to interrupt—with mere words—the comforting tones borne to us on the summer breeze: the hum of the bees, the sweet songs of the birds, the soft lowing of cattle, and a single-engine plane high above us. My mind is relaxed—maybe too relaxed. I'll think of something before we head home. *I can't let Jed's story appetite pass unsatisfied ... maybe an object lesson from something we've seen today.*

A cloud blocks the sun; the coolness in the wake of its shadow lures us further down the road. I stop to study a dilapidated farmhouse that seems out of harmony with the rest of the well-manicured neighborhood.

A straggly fence surrounds the cluttered yard. Unmatched sections of pallets and plywood form a zig-zagged border that nature has attempted to beautify with blue morning glories. Scattered unevenly across the front portion of the yard are rusty car parts, discarded washing machines, and numerous unrecognizable gadgets that the inhabitants of the house must consider valuable. Is the house even inhabited? It looks like it could be used as a Halloween haunt or something my parents might have attempted to rescue during their successful remodeling career.

"Whoever lives here sure loves animals," Jed remarked.

"They're having difficulty keeping up with their chores," I mutter. Assorted animals are cross-fenced into corners or penned in homemade cages. There are several chickens, a couple of goats, a pony, numerous rabbits, maybe a dozen cats, and at least three dogs.

"Mom!" Jed shouts, pointing excitedly toward a wrecked vehicle. "It's Champ!"

Instead of the beautiful yard in which I had pictured him, our noble friend is lying in the concave roof of a wrecked and rusty car. His head and ears flat down, his eyes half closed, as if the weight of the thick rope with which he is tied has robbed him of all his energy.

"Hey, Champ!" Jed hollers across the road.

At the sound of Jed's voice, the dog opens his eyes, his head and ears quickly rise, and then, despite his demeaning imprisonment and impoverished surroundings, he stands up and begins furiously wagging his tail. The transformation is extraordinary to behold. I actually did not recognize him until he stood up.

Guarding Instinct

"Can I go to him, Mommy? Please?" Jed's plea tugs at my heart, but from out of the distant past I hear my little brother's warning and feel the jaws of another German shepherd upon whose property I had trespassed.

In answer to Jed's request for a story, I recall that very time when I was protected from serious injury.

"German shepherds have territorial instincts, Jed." I caution. "Venturing onto Champion's turf would challenge his protective nature. He knows you, that's true, but he's on guard duty now, and we'd be trespassing on his turf."

"Something scary happened to me when I was about your age," I continued, as we headed homeward. "That helped me understand the guarding instinct of shepherd dogs. Like you, I was born loving animals, but my little brother feared everything with four legs. Walking to school together one day, we saw a beautiful silver German shepherd. Paying no heed to Doug's terrified warnings about the 'Guard Dog On Duty' sign that was posted on the gate, I climbed the long flight of steps up to where the big dog was lying on the front porch, his paws over the edge of the first step. The closer I got, the bigger he appeared, until he looked as big as a lion to my young eyes. I should have respected his deep growl and steady gaze, but I had never yet had a bad experience with a dog. So, when I reached out to pet this massive animal, my naïve outlook was severely modified.

"That huge silver beast grabbed my little nine-year-old arm in his teeth and pressed down hard with his powerful jaws! He could have inflicted serious injury. Without moving from his position, instead of tossing me about like a rag doll, he gradually released his vice-grip with another warning growl.

"When he released me, I slowly backed down the stairs and through his gate—my eyes never losing track of his. Though my skin was scuffed a bit and my arm was bruised for a few days, I received no puncture wounds because my heavy winter coat prevented serious injury."

"Wow, Mom! Why did he do that to you? You weren't going to hurt him!"

"Many dogs—especially German shepherds—have inborn guarding instincts," I answered. "When they are on their own turf,

> *Many dogs—especially German shepherds—have inborn guarding instincts.*

you must not cross their line. . They can't speak to us in our language, so it's up to us to learn their language and respect their boundaries. When they are on our turf, we can teach them to obey our rules, and that is called obedience training."

"What do we call it when we are on their turf?"

"Common sense."

When we are nearly back home, Jed breaks the silence with a lifetime conclusion. "I will *never* choose to live where animals can't run free."

"Maybe we can visit with Champ's family sometime when they're home. OK?" I said, fully intending to keep that promise. It was obvious that boy and dog had become perfectly bonded.

> *They can't speak to us in our language, so it's up to us to learn their language and respect their boundaries.*

> The intelligence displayed by many dumb animals approaches
> so closely to human intelligence that it is a mystery.
> The animals see and hear and love and fear and suffer.
> They use their organs far more faithfully than
> many human beings use theirs.
> They manifest sympathy and tenderness toward
> their companions in suffering.
> Many animals show an affection for those
> who have charge of them,
> far superior to the affection shown by some of the human race.
> They form attachments for man which are not broken without
> great suffering to them.
> (Ellen G. White, *The Ministry of Healing*, p. 315)

The next day, Champ tapped on the door during breakfast. After Jed fed him a piece of whole wheat toast with peanut butter, they went outside to explore distant horizons within range of my kitchen window.

I wish that this special bond of friendship between my son and this beautiful dog could last. I will visit Champ's family someday soon. There will be time, on some other, less busy day.

Every day delivers a new excuse to ignore my promise; a letter to write, housework to do, homeschool, a garden to weed, flowers to smell.

News from a Far Country

One hot summer afternoon in late August, Jere returns from the restaurant, lays an envelope on the kitchen table, gives me a hug, and commences an astounding announcement.

"Read it, Linda!" he says, smiling broadly enough to show the dimples he passed on to our son. "I've been accepted for that teaching position in microbiology that I applied for at Loma Linda University School of Medicine!"

It takes a while for me to absorb the information. "But … but, do we *want* to live in *California?*"

"No, it's just for a while," he says, gesturing helplessly, palms up and shoulders raised. "It's where the job is, and we are in need of some funds to rebuild our savings. They want us to come down to sign the contract and find a place to live … ASAP!"

Just when I'm not ready, the shadows descend. But am I ever ready for shadows? When *would* I welcome clouds? Change is no friend of mine.

> Oh, for living, active, faith!
> We need it; we must have it, or we shall faint
> and fail in the day of trial.
> The darkness that will then rest upon our path
> must not discourage us,
> or drive us to despair.
> It is the veil with which God covers His glory
> when He comes to impart rich blessings.
> We should know this by our past experience.
> In that day when God has a controversy with His people,
> this experience will be a source of comfort and hope.
> (Ellen G. White, *Christian Experience and Teaching*, p. 190)

What about Jed's friendship with Champion? How will we break the news to our son? Now that he has a friend with which to share his waking hours, Jed has a permanent smile on his face.

I need not wonder for long. I can tell by his pained expression when Jed comes around the corner into the kitchen that he already knows the sacrifice he is being called upon to make.

Chapter 3

The Incredible Gift

Do not fear to hope, even when hoping seems hopeless.

> My life is but a weaving between my Lord and me;
> I may not choose the colors—He knows what they should be.
> For He can view the colors upon the upper side
> While I can see them only upon this under side.
>
> Not 'til the loom is silent and the shuttles cease to fly
> Will God unroll the pattern and explain the reason why
> The dark threads were as needful in the Weaver's skillful hand
> As the threads of gold and silver in the pattern which He planned.
> —Anonymous

Time is ice—the moment of truth frozen. The three of us look at each other in silence. There is nothing to say. Not one of us wants to move from the niche we have carved out in this little corner of the Pacific Northwest, but the offer of employment to a well-paid position that includes moving expenses and medical coverage appears providential.

Finally breaking the silence, Jere says quietly, "I'd like to leave tomorrow morning."

"Tomorrow?" I repeat, choking on the words. "But I can't possibly pack that quickly!"

"No, not for moving," he explains, "just to go down to Loma Linda to find housing."

It was a mild reprieve. I didn't know it at the time, but this short interaction with Jere was only the first of numerous adrenalin rushes that would, by a unique series of events, engrave the next few days upon my soul. Like an intricate etching on crystal, this spiritual art form was subject to breakage, with each gouge more painful than the one before.

Thankfully, Champion has gone home for the day, so I can avoid his golden-eyed inquest—at least until we return. I turn my attention to packing for a quick trip to California.

Save for the books I bring along to share, the two-day trip to California is quiet. Thoughts run deep. Four days later, we're back home in Brush Prairie. Jere has signed the contract with Loma Linda University Medical Center as well as a rental agreement for a comfortable home in Mentone, a little less crowded city not far from Loma Linda though definitely not in the country.

While Jere ties off loose ends at work, Jed and I begin stuffing boxes with our household goods and packing them into our old school bus that has served as moving van and motor home during our southern sojourn of the past three years. During our packing days, Jed receives not one visit from Champion until the very last day.

The Hardest Part

On the morning of August 8, 1986, we hear Champion tap on the door at breakfast time. In his usual tour of the house, he encounters unfamiliar disorganization throughout. The empty rooms, unswept floors, half-filled boxes, and large plastic bags stuffed with soft toys that smell like his good friend are cause for alarm. He returns from his tour to stand in the kitchen doorway, head cocked sideways, a quizzical expression on his face. He glances at Jed, then holds my gaze, again tipping his head sideways, and then lies down with his head on his paws, deep in contemplation. His amber eyes follow me, though He does not move. He does not go outside to play with Jed. He just stares at me—wherever I go—all day. If I could, I would tell him, but I don't know his language.

The house is finally clean. I fold the flaps together on the last boxes, label them, and then snap the lid shut on my felt pen. I can feel Jed and Champ's eyes on me. Save for a couple of discarded boxes and a half-inflated Mylar balloon hovering beside them, Jed and Champ lay side-by-side in the empty living room.

Jed looks up at me, his blue eyes pooling. "The hardest part of moving to California is leaving Champ, right, Mommy?"

I kneel beside him wanting to kiss away his pain, but Jed early established his preference for verbal validation over sloppy sentimentalism. I nod silently and squeeze his shoulder. How does a mother explain away life's injustices? I have taught my son to believe in a loving God, yet I can offer him no immediate balm. His question hangs in the air between us like his deflated birthday balloon—tangible, but unfixable.

> *It just isn't fair; Jed has lost Tramp, and now he will have to leave behind his new best friend. What can I do? Help, please, Lord!*

His connection to Champion, like the once beautiful orb, looks hopeless. I reach for the balloon, absently squish it, and watch the flower puff up like new. Oh, that my hands might perform this kind of resuscitation on Jed's broken heart! Will he be permanently deflated, disillusioned, and afraid to dream? As much as I want to voice some hope, the right words do not come. I reach toward my son. When he pulls away, the unused hug transforms itself into an unspoken prayer.

Here is a little boy and a wonderful dog who love each other, Lord. Tonight, they will be separated forever. It just isn't fair; Jed has lost Tramp, and now he will have to leave behind his new best friend. What can I do? Help, please, Lord! Why does life have so many shadows?

My mind returns to the image of the old farmhouse and Champion's wrecked-car doghouse. He deserves better. Gently, I hold the soft muzzle in my hand. Champion looks into my eyes, then lays his head across Jed's legs, sighs deeply, and closes his eyes. He knows—He really knows—and he is grieving!

Champion Leads the Way

With supper finished, Jere stows the heavier boxes in the bus. Champion has stayed much later than usual. He has refused to eat anything Jed has offered him all day. We all look at each other knowing that the time has come for Champion's final exit. Jere nods toward the door. I open it, hoping my voice will not fail me.

"Please go home, Champ," I request.

For the first time in all the months we'd known him, the dog refused to obey. Maybe my voice was not strong enough. I glance toward Jere. I see something barely more than tiredness in those blue eyes, but he still has the strength to maintain discipline. He nods at me again. If I don't accomplish this, he will.

"Go home!" I attempt to sound firm. Champion does not budge, just stares out into the darkness. I turn on the porch light, hoping to make the night appear friendlier.

"Champion, go home!" I repeat, louder and more firmly. Champion cowers against the blow he is prepared to withstand. I had never struck him, but someone must have. I press my hands against his backside, but he plants his front feet firmly against the threshold. He is too heavy for me to lift. I stand, hands on hips, eyes brimming with tears of sadness too deep for any other kind of expression.

The voice of reason takes a deep breath and dives into the depths of my despair. One at a time, little bubbles of thought rise to the surface of my troubled mind. My change of attitude causes Champ to look back at me. Am I imagining it, or is he trying to tell me something? I look at the ceiling, more to shut out those golden eyes than to see the handwriting that I wish I could see up there.

Lord, I just can't do what I have to do. Champion deserves better—he doesn't even have a decent doghouse. I think he's telling me that he wants to be with us, but ... that's impossible! Oh, Lord, isn't there something I can do?

The image of Champ's home is stuck in my brain. I can't think of anything else! My heart tells me to take Champ home. I should have tried to connect with his family a month ago when we "accidentally" discovered where he lived instead of waiting until this last possible minute to do so.

"May I take Champ home in the car, Jere?" I ask, not really expecting him to agree. We are all tired, and it's after 9 pm. From his perch on the last box of books, Jere closes his eyes, nods imperceptibly, sighs, and holds the car keys out to me. This move to California is harder on him than either Jed or me, and although it has taken longer for his own "Tramp wound" to heal, I know that he likes Champion.

"Be sure to leave our address card with his owners," he says, as he heaves the last of the heaviest packing boxes up onto his strong shoulder. "That way, if they ever have to get rid of him, well, maybe they can ... call us ... or something." But what good will it do to leave our address when we will soon be a thousand miles away?

Amazingly, Champion follows me willingly, jumping into the front seat of our old station wagon for the first time as if he'd ridden this way for years. I square my shoulders and sniff away my tears as we back out of the driveway. It will never do to visit Champ's folks with red eyes! I reach through the darkness to touch, one last time, the comforting softness of that noble head as we begin our final journey together.

"I truly wish you could go with us, Champ." He lays a paw on my knee. I sense him looking at me through the dark shadows of the night.

Driving slowly along the country lane, I become more and more concerned that I might not recognize Champ's home in the dark. I only saw it once. Then the thought strikes me—what if I *do* find it? Talking to strangers is way out of my comfort zone. My foot eases off of the accelerator.

Then another thought sears its way into my heart—maybe I've already waited too long! I accelerate.

Lord, I know it's late, but please help me find that house! If You open the way, I really will talk ... but You will have to put the words in my mouth. You know how clumsy I am with my words.

Right at the peak of desperation, as I am certain I have already passed Champ's home, a familiar accumulation of unmatched fences suddenly looms into the headlights. I pull into the yard, switch off my lights, kill the engine, and then look toward the house. It looks uninhabited—ghostly, actually. Every single window is dark. I'm too late!

The Song

Cold dread engulfs me. With a heavy sigh I lean my head against the steering wheel, close my eyes, and heave a deep sigh. I will *never* know Champion's family now! Then, unexplainably I hear a childhood melody slipping into my heart. The words come through as clearly as if Mamma was sitting in the backseat singing the one song that has always made me run away in dread. I am engulfed by the haunting lyrics of the old country song by Red Foley about another Shepherd from long ago ...

Old Shep
When I was a boy and Old Shep was a pup,
O'er hills and meadows we'd roam.
Just a boy and his dog, we were both full of fun
We grew up together that way.

I remember the day, at the old swimming hole,
When I would have drowned without doubt—
Shep was right there, to the rescue he came,
He jumped in and helped pull me out.

So the years rolled along, and, at last, he grew old—
His eyesight was fast growing dim.
Then one day the doctor looked at me and said,
"I can't do no more for him, Jim."

With a hand that was trembling I picked up my gun.
I aimed it at Shep's faithful head—
I just couldn't do it—I wanted to run,
And I wished that they'd shoot me instead.

I went to his side and sat on the ground.
He laid his head on my knee.
I stroked the best pal that a man ever found.
I cried so I scarcely could see.

Old Sheppie, he knew he was going to go,
For he reached out and licked at my hand.
He looked up at me just as much as to say,
"We're parting but I understand."

Now Old Sheppie is gone where the good doggies go,
And no more will Shep and I roam.
But if dogs have a heaven there's one thing I know,
Old Shep has a wonderful home.

The Light

The song in my memory comes to an end. I open my leaking eyes and blink in disbelief! Wiping my tears, I look again. There is a light in a window! A shadow plays across the crooked window blind upstairs. Grotesque and misshapen, a few seconds earlier the silhouette would have frightened me, but not now. Maybe I'm not too late! With my heart in my throat, I swipe once more at my tears with the back of my hand and step quickly from the car. Champion leads the way up the rickety front steps and sits down beside me like a well-trained service dog, looking from me to the doorknob and back to me again, as if to say, "Go ahead! Tap on the door! If you do that, it will actually open!"

Gathering courage from his trusting eyes, I double my fist. Again, fear threatens to paralyze me. Will my voice work? If it does, what will I say? I practice speaking, soft and repetitive, in varying tones, clearing my throat, like one does when the phone rings too early in the morning—"Hell-o, hello … hello?"

As always, my throat is painfully constricted, as if unseen hands are squeezing my neck. This is the way it has always been for me, for as long as I can remember, and I don't know why. Spoken words seem inversely proportionate to my need of them—the more important the subject and the greater the pressure, the fewer the words that find their escape from my lips. Like the broken debris that causes an ice-jam on a northern river in the springtime, my words swirl in a whirlpool, dammed somewhere between my brain and my vocal cords.

I wish desperately that I had my Mother's gift of speech and song. Then I could easily tell these folks about my wonderful son who loves their beautiful dog, about my loving husband who faithfully provides for our needs, and that, if ever they need to find a home for Champion, all they have to do is call us. I would tell them that I will personally guarantee that Champion never goes hungry or is mistreated.

My arm falls limp. I just can't knock. If I do, then I will have to talk. Oh, but I *must!* I tighten my fist again, close my eyes, and pray that the light in the window is shining from a warm heart.

The Answer

I'm not sure that I ever knocked on that door. When I open my eyes, the porch light is on and the door is open. I shiver in anticipation and dread. It's time to say something.

I needn't have worried about my speech disability. From the time that door opens, nothing more than a nod of my head at strategic intervals will be required. I extend my hand to the tiny woman who grabs it and propels me inside her domain.

"Hi! I'm Leta! You must be the lady who likes Champ ... enough to feed him pancakes! Yes, my boys have heard about you and your son at school from the boys in your trailer court."

Though I manage to tell her my name, Leta fills every conversational gap. I detect no condemnation in her voice, though she has every right to be accusatory. After all, our feeding of her dog has, no doubt, contributed to his wanderlust.

"I'm *so* happy you've come, Linda!" Leta clasps her thin hands together and smiles. "This is *so* amazing! I was just thinking about you! In fact, I was just now praying that you would come ..."

How could you have been thinking about me, Leta? We've never met!

She pushes a dilapidated wooden chair toward me. Champion stands between us wearing the same expression he has carried all day, as if he wants to talk. Leta strokes his head.

"We missed you today, Champ!" Champion glances up at her, wags his tail politely, then sits down near me, his eyes, once again, riveted on mine.

"You're a Christian, aren't you, Linda?" Leta smiles. I nod. "Good, it would be difficult to explain to an unbeliever what I am about to tell you." She smooths her faded pink housecoat, folds her hands atop the table between us, and takes a deep breath as if to organize her thoughts.

"Not long ago, I was at the end of my rope. My husband had abandoned the boys and me. We were better off without him, but survival became a burden. I had strayed far from the faith of my childhood. My grandmother raised me as a Seventh-day Adventist, and the farther I got from God, the less I desired to return." Tears filled her eyes. She pointed toward the ceiling, "I went so far astray as to wonder if *He* even existed!"

"It was at the very lowest point in my life that my youngest son, Alvin, was kidnapped. The police searched for him without success. Having nowhere else to turn, I finally made a deal with God. For the first time in years, I prayed a real prayer." Leta's voice is emotional. Tears glitter in her eyes before she bows her head and clasps her hands as if to re-enact her prayer.

"Lord, if You will just return Alvin to me, I will know that You are real. I will return to You." She lifts her head triumphantly, her hands open as if to collect the blessing bestowed.

"Believe me, Linda, when I tell you that God opened the windows of heaven! I couldn't keep up with the miracles that happened after I prayed that prayer! Within minutes my phone rang. The police had just closed in on a new lead. Within hours I was holding little Alvin in my arms! In a flood of gratefulness, my faith returned to me. I have a loving church family now. I recently met a wonderful Christian man who loves me and my boys. So many answers to prayer! Our wedding is just a few days away!" She points at me, her dark eyes sparkling.

"That's where *you* come in, Linda! Two weeks from today we'll be moving to Milwaukee, Oregon. We won't be able to have any animals in our new home there. Just now, I was upstairs praying about Champion when you came to my mind. I decided to go to the trailer court to try to find you tomorrow morning to ask if you could take him, and here you are, right in my living room! If *that's* not a direct answer to prayer!" She leans forward in anticipation.

I was so enraptured by Leta's story that I think I forgot to blink for a while. My eyes burn, goose bumps leapfrog up and down my spine. I want to accept the invitation, but I can't utter a sound. My head won't move. I'm paralyzed.

"You *can* take him, can't you?" Leta begs.

At this, I sense the presence of angels in the room. It's as if warm oil is being poured over my head, down my whole body. I tingle from head to toe. The constriction in my throat is released. I open my mouth to speak, but my thoughts intervene.

Wait! Champion could run away at the first rest stop tomorrow and be killed! We can't give this wonderful dog the home he really deserves—Tramp was killed in our care. I'd need a leash, collar, food bowl and water bucket by tomorrow … and what if he gets heat stroke … California is hot in August. And what about our new place?

In the midst of my mental gymnastics, Champion rises from a sitting position to stand directly in front of me, lays his head in my lap and places his right paw on my left knee, his golden eyes gripping mine. Finally, I get what he's been trying to tell me.

Champ! You've known all along. Leta can't keep you. You've chosen us!

Leta slices the silence with an ultimatum. "If you can't take him, I'll have to put him down. I hate to do it—he's such a *good* dog. He just needs a family who will give him …"

I hear Mamma singing again, "… *and if dogs have a heaven, there's one thing I know, Old Shep has* …" My heart attempts to connect with my vocal cords.

"… a wonderful home!" I am finally able to blurt out.

"Yes!" Leta's fists pierce the air with a victory sign. "You can give him that!"

But when I open my mouth to reassure her, a high-pitched wail pierces the hallowed atmosphere of sacred praise.

"No, no!" The scream is not coming from my mouth but from a dilapidated couch in a darkened corner of the living room. "Not my Champy!" sobs the little boy that emerges from a pile of covers, dragging his well-worn blankie across the threadbare carpet. He's heading straight for me, but Leta reaches out and muffles his sobs against her bosom.

Champion removes his paw from my knee, solemnly averts his eyes, slinks toward the door and lies down with his nose pressing tightly against the crack of air at the threshold. His ears are flat against his head, presumably to stifle the cries of the loved one he must leave behind.

"Champy! Don't go 'way fwum me!" the boy sobs loudly, his beloved blankie falling to the floor as he attempts to escape.

"Alvin, be quiet now." Leta sooths, empathetic tears pooling in her eyes. "We can't have pets where we're moving, remember? We've prayed together that God would provide good homes for them." Little Alvin looks up at his mother, hiccups, and nods imperceptibly. "Your Champion is so *special* that God chose to send this lady tonight to answer our prayer right while I was praying about finding a good home for him!"

Alvin glances warily at me. With an uneven sigh he places his thumb in his mouth and lays his head, directed away from me, in his mother's lap. Leta cups her hand and covers his ear.

"Champion is yours," she gestures pointedly with her free hand while mouthing her message to me. "If he's not here in the morning I'll know he is with you. Go now …" she waves, smiling through her tears, "… and God go with you!"

"My Champion"

Destiny has called. I take a deep breath praying that my body will move. Champion looks back at me. One of the angels in the room must have given me strength. I leave the address card on the table. As I approach the door, Champion assumes a sitting position and stares at the doorknob. Laying one hand on his head, I open the door and look back toward Leta.

She is smiling at me through her tears and rocking her little boy. I mouth my thankfulness and blow her a kiss. Her warm smile, bedewed with sacrificial tears, follows me out the door.

The midsummer darkness is a soft shawl. Champion presses companionably against me all the way to the car, then jumps into the passenger seat and offers me his paw. With a teary smile, I seal the deal of a lifetime.

Yes, Lord! Thank You! This is the way every chapter in every book should end! I will never again lose my grip on faith. Never! Not after tonight! Why is it so hard to trust that all things really will work out for the good? I love You, Lord! Oh, thank You! Thank You! Thank You! This is just too good to be true!

We ride home in silence until I pull into the driveway. "Well, Champ, wherever we are, you'll always be home!" Trotting ahead of me, he taps one final time on the kitchen door. I open it for him, my heart swollen with joy to share the good news with the men in my life.

Despite the lateness of the hour, Jere and Jed are still awake and sitting in the empty living room. Their attitude reminds me that we haven't had worship yet! When I walk into the living room with Champion, Jed stares at the dog without touching him, not daring to hope. He looks at me, eyebrows arched, his blue eyes questioning. I open my mouth, hoping that something intelligent will emerge. But there is a big lump that the words will have to squeeze through.

"He's ours ... we can ... have him."

"Champy!" Jed embraces his friend. "My Champion!"

My heart will never be cold again. Who can ever doubt a compassionate God who delivers such joy? In His hands, He holds all good things. How can I ever doubt His goodness?

Big Problem

Jere is not smiling. His next words paralyze my diaphragm and stifle my breath.

"What about the rental agreement?" he asks. "You know—the one with those big red letters across the top. Remember—the one we just signed in front of Rosie that spelled out NO PETS?"

I am smothered by dread, fear, and disappointment. My little flag of faith wilts. How could I have forgotten such an important detail? Impossibility binds my hands, my heart, and my voice. I watch my dreams fall to ashes at my feet. I cannot lift my head. This is a legal problem. Moms can't solve legal problems. I am enveloped, completely, in hopelessness, for there is no way out of this dilemma.

> Above the distractions of the earth He sits enthroned;
> all things are open to His divine survey;
> and from His great and calm eternity
> He orders that which His providence sees best.
> (Ellen G. White, *The Ministry of Healing*, p. 417)

Chapter 4

Unexpected Advice

When there's no other way, God touches hearts.

> Black may be the clouds about you
> And your future may seem grim,
> But don't let your nerve desert you;
> Keep yourself in fighting trim.
> If the worst is bound to happen,
> Spite of all that you can do,
> Running from it will not save you,
> See it through.
> —Edgar A. Guest in "See It Through"

"Oh, Jere!" I groan, collapsing at his feet. "Is there nothing we can do?"

"You'll have to phone Rosie."

The illumination that energized me in Leta's living room and on the drive home with our heavenly gift is gone. My strength is weakness. My promise to never again lose my grip on faith has been sucked into the hideous vacuum of doubt. My strength is weakness. My promise to never again lose my grip on faith has been sucked into the hideous vacuum of

> *My strength is weakness. My promise to never again lose my grip on faith has been sucked into the hideous vacuum of doubt.*

doubt. Never before have I experienced such extreme heights and depths of emotion as I have in the past hour; the desperation, the direct answer to prayer, and now the dashing of my hopes. Champion, on the other hand, wears the same expression of trusting expectancy that he has worn since the moment he entered our lives.

"Would *you* please call Rosie?" I beg. Jere silently shakes his head.

"Well, maybe we can just *take* Champ ... pray that when we get there, she'll ... like him?" I bargain.

"No, that would be unfair—to both Rosie and Champ," he insists. "You'll have to see this through."

"But ... the phone ... it's disconnected now. I *can't* call!"

"Go down to Pat's—this has to be resolved before we leave in the morning."

"But ... it's so, so late," I protest weakly.

Jere nods his head toward the door and blinks slowly. My last argument falls on deaf ears. Shoulders slumped, I head back out into the night.

Shadows of the Soul

I am immediately wrapped in a suffocating shroud as I close the door behind me. Cold stars swim in an indigo sea far above me. I shiver in spite of the warmth of the summer night. Stumbling in the shadows, I weep as much for the sweetness of my experience as much as for the bitterness of what will surely happen as a result of Jere's honesty. Too soon Pat's door looms before me. Holding my breath, I form a fist with my right hand.

Wait, Linda! Will you be able to speak? What will you say? How can you make Pat understand how important it is to be able to take Champion with you to California? You are completely at the mercy of Pat and Rosie! O, Lord ... help!

I unfold my fist and tap lightly on the door with my fingernail, half-hoping Pat will not hear. Amazingly, it's as if she has been anticipating my late-night arrival.

"It's you, Linda!" Pat steps out onto the porch and pulls the door shut behind her. "Why, whatever-r- is w-r-rrong, m'dear-r-ry?" I blubber my burdens into her ample bosom. Surely nothing I say will make any sense to her. When I finish, she holds me at arm's length.

"Well, that's *good* news, it is, isn't it?" There's a lilt in her brogue and a twinkle in her eye.

"You do like Champ. So, you must be cr-r-rying for-r-r joy? We'll get this sor-r-ted out. Don-cha lose hope, now!" She herds me into her kitchen where I am enveloped in the comforting aroma of fresh-baked cinnamon rolls.

"Her-r-re, give me that number-r-r!" She smooths Jere's moist and crumpled note onto her kitchen counter, quickly dials the number, then thrusts the receiver at me before I lose the courage I don't have. My heart rate races faster with each unanswered ring.

Oh dear, it's so late! I hope Rosie's not asleep. Lord, I hardly know what to say. I ...

"Hello?" (Rosie doesn't sound sleepy.)

"Hi. Uh, Rosie? This is Linda. I know it's late, and I'm so sorry to bother you."

"I'm a late-night person, Linda," she lilts, erasing my apology, "and I'm *so* glad you called! I dialed your number today, but apparently your phone had already been disconnected. Someone broke into your house here last night. I wanted to let you know."

My voice has taken leave ... again.

"Are you there?"

"M-m-m-m ...?" I don't know what to say ... again.

"I'm not sure how you feel about getting a *dog*," Rosie continues, "but I think it would be a great preventive measure to discourage further break-ins. The yard is fully fenced, you know. A German shepherd would be an excellent choice, but it's a little late to be too choosy. You're probably leaving in the morning, right? Maybe you can find one when you get down here. There's a rescue pound not far from us."

"But," I swallow hard. "But ... um ... didn't we sign a ... a ... *no pet contract?*"

"Oh, *that!*" she snorts. "That's printed on *all* my agreements. Doesn't mean a *thing*. Just a formality. So, you're not *opposed* to getting a dog then?"

I pucker my lips, trying to stifle the uncontrollable giggle that I feel welling up in my stomach. Disappointment and ecstasy collide. Once again, euphoria reigns supreme. How can one body endure such an emotional roller coaster as I have been on tonight? A deep breath steadies my diaphragm—just a little. Is it enough to control my voice?

"We can try ..." I hedge. "And thanks, Rosie ... *thanks a lot!*"

"Have a safe trip, Linda," she chirps, "and God bless."

"He has, Rosie," I hear myself saying, as I return the receiver to our smiling landlady, "He *really* has."

> Ministering angels are waiting about the throne
> to instantly obey the mandate of Jesus Christ
> to answer every prayer offered in earnest, living faith.
> (Ellen G. White, *Selected Messages*, book 2, p. 377)

Song in the Night

There is music in my soul as the velvet comforter of the summer night enfolds me. I can't recall hearing a symphony begin with a dial tone since the first time Jere asked me out for a drive. The stars are almost within touching distance as they illuminate and ignite my experience of the night, experiences such as God must set aside for a privileged few.

I feel incredibly small in this newfound knowledge, this new assurance that I am a fractional part of an immense movement—the orchestra of the universe. Nothing I have done qualifies me to play the tiniest part; nevertheless, as I behold the glory of the stars, the harmonies become more intense until the wild beating of my thankful heart can hardly hold the joy. The heavenly song is all there—complete with lyrics—Jed's wish to adopt Champion, my desperation, and Leta's heartfelt prayer request. Even little Alvin's little dissonance and the marimba of the rental agreement added to the glory of the concert. The music was orchestrated somewhere far above, in that land where there is neither pain nor tears nor sorrow nor crying at all. The lyrics, including the joy of this score, are so clear to me in this moment. We are all pre-scripted. I strain to listen. I can hear some of the words.

> What heavenly music steals over the sea!
> Entrancing the senses like sweet melody!
> 'Tis the voice of the angels borne soft on the air
> For me they are singing their welcome I hear.
> —James White, "What Heavenly Music"

This incredible arrangement was carefully computed somewhere out past the shadows of night, above the clouds, the moon, and even the stars. Angels carefully calculated the time and place for the crossing of the paths of two praying mothers who could easily have missed a grand opportunity to be part of tonight's poignant presentation in the southwest corner of Washington. And the orchestration started when the prayers of two mothers who desperately loved their sons, ascended heavenward.

> It is impossible to estimate the power
> of a praying mother's influence.
> She acknowledges God in all her ways.
> She takes her children before the throne
> of grace and presents them to Jesus,
> pleading for His blessing upon them.
> The influence of those prayers is to
> those children as "a wellspring of life."
> These prayers, offered in faith,
> are the support and strength of the Christian mother.
> (Ellen G. White, *The Adventist Home*, p. 266)

A Prayer Away

Perhaps even praying mothers are too involved with the things of earth to be in tune with Providence. The gift—a dog named Champion—anxiously awaits the time of bestowal. Having learned some canine language, one mother detects a message forming in the golden eyes of the gift. With dim perception, she senses the beginning of a song and tries to follow the melody but stumbles in the darkness. Yet, it is within that very darkness that the song is born. To hear the harmonies of heaven within the shadows of night requires a faith that can't let go. Despondency is not an option when the soul becomes quiet enough to hear even the faintest whisper of hope.

> When every other voice is hushed, and in quietness
> we wait before Him,
> the silence of the soul makes more distinct the voice of God.
> (Ellen G. White, *The Desire of Ages*, p. 363)

    Lord, how many threads of coincidence does it take to weave a miracle? How often do I miss the melodies of heaven? Is there music in the stars? Maybe I just have to keep looking up?

    Miraculously, my insurmountable problem, Rosie's "NO PETS" policy, is a happy memory. How I wish now that Jere and Jed could have shared the incredible journey with me tonight! What a story I have to tell them! Will I be able to recapture even a small portion of the pathos I have experienced?

    Floating on faith and gratefulness, I do not stumble on my homeward journey, feeling as if I will never stumble again. Stepping lightly into our own little pool of porch light for the last time, I quietly open the door, turn off the porch light switch, and inspect the ranks. Jed is in his sleeping bag, his arm draped across his Champion. Champ lifts his head to acknowledge my presence. I caress his head and close the door.

When Every Other Voice is Hushed

I softly step down the hallway to our bedroom, my heart pumping furiously with the excitement of the evening. I have a desperate need.

I quietly open the bedroom door, where Jere is sleeping. I kneel beside our mattress, the last article of furniture that we will load in the morning crowning a carefully squared pile of boxes just behind the driver's seat. Once more our trusty old school bus will become a motor home for cross-country travel. Although I still don't want to go to California, at least our family is complete—now that we don't have to leave Champion behind. What a story!

Jere's ability to listen is one of the traits that first drew me to him. He'll surely want to hear how this phone call turned out! Time pressures won't allow me to tell the whole story in the morning to be able to savor the delicious details. Besides, it's still so fresh and warm—like the aroma of whole wheat bread baking in a wood cook stove, the mixture of smoke and grain, yeast and sweetness, all rising together to fill its purpose.

We will be driving separate vehicles for three exhausting days. I unplug the night light, undress in the darkness, and snuggle into bed, in need of Jere's warmth after my evening escapade, aching for release.

"Guess what?" I whisper. "Rosie was *hoping* we would bring a dog!"

"M-m-m," he mumbles.

"Want to hear the juicy details?"

"M-m-m-miles to go ... before we sleep ... tell me tomorrow ... 'kay?"

"Okay."

I try to sleep, but the music of this wondrous night rings in my ears, my heart, my whole being. If only I could find a notebook, I could record some of the facets of this story while I can still feel the warmth of the glow.

Lord, some might claim that this was all mere coincidence. I know better. I will always know better. Even if not one other person hears this story, even if no one else believes it, even if I never even write about it, I know that Champion is an incredible and unexpected but hoped for gift. I witnessed a miracle tonight—no, I participated in a miracle! I played a part in the concert! I heard the music and was somehow familiar with the score, as if it were orchestrated for me ... prewritten ... almost. Help me keep the melody in my heart.

Forcing my eyes closed, I picture myself once more in the driveway of Leta's old farmhouse, hoping for light. This time, with the eye of faith, I see the heads of at least two angels, bowed together and smiling at the success of their holy conspiracy. Angels (not unlike my own little eight-year-old-road-maker), gently contoured the paths of two praying mothers to intersect at the hour of utmost desperation, deciphering two dilemmas with a solution only heaven could have planned.

I see Champion, sitting quietly at my feet in Leta's living room until she pronounces her ultimatum. I feel him place his head in my lap and lift his right paw to press it onto my left knee. He had heard the beginning strains of the orchestra earlier in the day. He knew that his future hung in the balance. He understood what I had not.

As sleep overtakes me, Champion's message of trust is clear.

Unlike me, Champ never stooped to whine. He acted as if love were his motivation. As sleep overtakes me, Champion's message of trust is clear. He saw the notes on the cleft and paced his steps to follow the melody. If he could speak, or if I could hear and really understand, I, no doubt, would have heard his words of hope.

I ask myself how many times I have played Alvin's part and been left feeling empty when I could have chosen to intentionally believe that my loss was but a minor chord. Minor chords should merely help me look forward to the recurrence of the melody of praise that should be a permanent fixture in every Christian's heart. There are givers as well as gifts as we travel across the Sea of Life. Together, the doldrums of quiet waters, the high winds, and the tempestuous billows create a multiplicity of tones, but, without the play and counterplay, the movement is inconclusive. I can choose to listen to the music or to be deaf to the efforts of my Conductor's gift—everlasting praise. His ear is listening for the melody that I will return to Him under cover of darkness. I should have been able to sing that familiar melody in faith before I heard Rosie's blessed and most welcomed advice, but my heart is still too small to be able to remember that it is actually the presence of light that creates a shadow.

> We have nothing to fear for the future,
> except as we shall forget the way the Lord has led us,
> and His teaching in our past history.
> (Ellen G. White, *Christian Experience and Teachings*, p. 204)

When I see only shadows, the Light is not gone. The song of faith can only be sung in the darkness. I should know this; I should be able to grasp this truth; the darkest shadows are covered by the brightest light. Instead, I see the impossibility of what I am seeking that lies between the two.

Tomorrow we begin a lengthy journey. Surely the heavenly strains I've heard tonight will remind me, no matter where I go, that heaven is nearer earth than I ever thought possible. Tonight, God Himself appointed us a dog with a hearing heart.

Chapter 5

Learning Obedience

Gentle repetition is the key to learning obedience.

> There are peaceful roads in the way of life
> That take us where we want to go;
> But it's the unpaved paths in times of strife
> That teach us what we need to know.
> —L. Franklin

I must have slept. When I awaken, the shadows of night have been replaced. My waking thought is: Oh, to be able to believe that angels are orchestrating everything for my best good, even in the darkness.

For over a thousand miles, I follow the old yellow school bus that Jere has driven back and forth across the United States in the past three years, seeking employment and a place to call home—in Oregon, Tennessee, Washington, and now California. Champ's behavior is exemplary. It's as if he knows, understands, and has accepted his assignment—we are his niche, his assignment. He's a working dog. At rest stops, he knows what to do, quickly returning to the car in spite of the fact that he has no restraining leash. Champ's total dedication to our family—and most especially to Jed—intensifies my desire to train him so that he will obey despite any distraction.

Settling In

Shortly after arriving in Mentone, we are served with a summons to appear in court, pay a fine, or license Champion immediately. Our trip to the veterinarian proved an aggravation to Champ's aggression genes. To ascertain that Champ had been neutered, the doctor finally had to leave us in the examination room and close the door to a mere crack—just the width of his arm. From the shadows beyond, the timorous vet advised me to back Champion up to the crack in the door for the final leg of the exam. Champ did not appear to be the least bit proud of his new license, but Jed surely was!

With proof of his residency behind us, and an official tag displayed on his collar, I search for the best obedience class I can find in our area. By recommendation, I inquire about the Master K-9 class offered by Dan LeMaster, innocently oblivious of the discipline it will require of me.

The week before the class is to begin, I discover a pamphlet in the Mentone library explaining the Kohler method. I had purchased a 20-foot training leash that the booklet suggested, and then implemented the first few suggestions as we began walking Champ around the neighborhood. Fortunately, I was able to skip the part about training him to like his leash. He was always willing and anxious to take a walk. The standing order was incentive enough for Jed to accomplish his school lessons in record time, too.

Mustering the Troops

On a warm evening in November of 1986, dogs of every size, shape, and color converge on the manicured lawn at Mentone Park. Dan LeMaster's boot camp for dogs contains all the elements of drama: timing, discipline, variety, intensity—and comedy, should one dare to be caught smiling. LeMaster is at the center of the circle of dogs with their owners attached by a variety of leashes—everything from diamond-studded leather to a ragged rope. Many of us are still using the long training leash, a dead giveaway to our lack of experience.

Anyone can tell at a glance that LeMaster is all business. Had I known the degree of difficulty this training would represent, I would never have signed my name to the register that night. Under "Owner," I signed Jed's name, thinking I would assume the role of assistant trainer. LeMaster, however, vetoes that plan since Jed is only eight years old. Jed hands me the leash and gladly takes my place on the sidelines.

Like a commander surveying his troops, LeMaster's muscular arms are often folded across his chest, his keen eyes darting and his head unmoving. Our bungling disorder must be painful for him. He is a trainer of the best troop dogs in the world. Although a few in the circle appear to know the ropes, most of us have only one possible asset besides our dog—potential.

For the first exercise, our dogs are to walk beside us—on our left—then sit squarely beside us whenever we are commanded to stop. It's easy to spot the beginners; we are the ones tangled in our long training leash.

Toeing the Mark

"Walk your dogs!" LeMaster barks. "A dog that follows six inches ahead or behind his master is not being obedient. A dog who does not sit squarely is being disobedient. You are here to learn the meaning of *obedience*."

The rules are simple: first, speak your dog's name; second, speak your command—just once; third, never give your dog a command that you are not physically willing to follow through with, and, fourth, anything short of the first three steps will not accomplish the purpose of the class. Obedience apparently does not include coddling, begging, or bribery. No treats are allowed. Obedience is black and white. LeMaster sets the mark; we are to toe it—exactly.

Distributed at random among the beginners are a dozen or so well-trained purebreds that have already attended at least one obedience class.

These dogs have short leashes and sit quietly during our instructional rest stops. During these training interludes, I am distracted by the comical similarities and disparities between certain dogs and their owners.

The Don

By far the largest animal on opening night looks like a canine caricature of Don Quixote—a gigantic, painfully malnourished Wolfhound-Great Dane cross whose huge head droops as if his collar is made of lead. Large portions of his chest and back are bald. His coat, where there is fur, is rough, splotched with carnival colors from the Dane gene pool. His tail, mostly hairless, sticks straight out behind him, except for the last three inches that dangle limply earthward. Considering the slowness of the beast, I conclude that his tail must have been accidentally slammed in a door. I overheard his doting, petite owner, a veterinarian's assistant, telling a group of women how she had recently rescued the animal from an untimely death at the local animal shelter.

Ol' "Dane Quixote" may have desired to respond to his mistress, but he was just too weak to perform. Pulling him just once around the ring convinced the girl that neither of them was equal to the rigors that would be required. Some degree of unity might one day come to the incongruous pair, but it would be a while. I wondered if the young lady would be able to maintain her enthusiasm after she paid the cost of his food for a month or two. This team was the first of several to drop out of class that first night.

The Standards

I focus my attention on a pair of unruly but gorgeous Standard Poodles that are causing a distraction over on the far side. One of them is white and is as impeccably groomed as her peroxide blonde mistress. They look as if they have stepped from the pages of a fashion magazine. Perfectly matched—identical hair and fur, impeccably clean, and fashionably slender. The poodle wears a jeweled collar. The lady wears tall, white platform sandals, a white pantsuit, a diamond pendant, and a red silk scarf. Next to her stands a tall, dark, and handsome man who appears to be of Greek descent. He is dark-skinned, well-muscled, curly haired, and dressed in black. He handles a big black Standard Poodle sporting a thick, silver-studded black leather collar, matching the man's belt. The black pair is every bit as striking as the white pair. They are a picture-perfect team—this wife and her husband. It is obvious that the wife is the leader of the pack. She is their spokesperson.

LeMaster, however, is not impressed by appearances. For better control of their dogs, he asks the couple to replace their trendy collars with the required choke chain necklaces. The big dogs prance mindlessly around their glamorous owners. When the man-in-black attempts to modify his dog's behavior, I conclude that attending obedience class was his notion. It may well have been his last attempt at preserving both his sanity and his marriage. His wife allows him to coax, coddle, pet, and praise but not actually discipline the big black bundle of energy at his side.

LeMaster, extending his open hand toward the man, asks the husband if he can use Big Black for a demonstration. As the man in black strides purposefully toward LeMaster, a well-manicured hand catches the sleeve of his silk shirt.

"Wait!" commands the lady. "Will this hurt my baby?"

"Not *half* as much as these dogs will hurt your reputation if you let them continue to ignore you!" LeMaster barked back. "This is an obedience class! Do you want your dogs to learn to obey or not?"

"Well," she responded demurely, "Not if it *hurts!*"

Silence. The dark eyes of the husband bounce in uncertainty between his wife and his instructor. The lady nonchalantly inspects a nail. LeMaster waits, arm outstretched. Just when it appears that the man might close the gap by tossing the dog's leash across the remaining distance, Big Black jumps up on the man and begins making bold and unmannerly advances. Red of face, the man asks the dog in a strained voice, "Sit," then "down," and finally, "STOP!" The dog pays no heed. Just when we are convinced that the man's escape from the dog's embrace will conclude with the infliction of severe injury, the woman in white envelopes her precious "child" in a sympathetic hug. Grabbing the black leash, she pulls the dog off of her husband and shoots a dagger at LeMaster. "No, you may not demonstrate on our dogs," she huffs. "These are our babies, not your guinea pigs!"

"Then you will leave." LeMaster's jaw muscles are flexing but his voice is controlled. "Now."

The perfect family leaves together. The last image of them I have is of a red silk scarf streaming artistically from a white Cadillac as it disappears into a brilliant orange California sunset.

Pepsi

LeMaster redirects his attention toward a huge Doberman named Pepsi, whose whines have increased in volume until he can no longer be heard by the group straining to listen to him. The Dobi outweighs his diminutive handler by at least fifty pounds. Li, his tiny Asian mistress, has to actually reach up slightly to touch Pepsi's ears. Like the Don and his mistress, the two are as unsuited as a cotton rope on a satin gown.

"Pepsi! Qui-ET!" demands LeMaster. Pepsi licks his chops and repositions himself like a hen hunkering on her nest. He sits still for about ten seconds of soothing silence. Then the whining gradually increases until LeMaster is fairly shouting again to make himself heard.

"You must gain your dog's respect by acquiring and maintaining his attention." For emphasis, LeMaster's fist impacts his hand with increased frequency and severity. "Some trainers use treats, but this is absolutely UNNECESSARY …" LeMaster shuts one eye, whips around and points his finger at the Pepsi as if looking down a rifle barrel. "Pep-SI! QUIET!"

Nostrils flaring, LeMaster stalks toward Pepsi and exhales in front of him. Pepsi sits in silent awe. Nothing happens. LeMaster must be counting to ten. When he speaks his tone is almost gentle.

"Don't you think he might be just a little big for you, Li?"

"I need a watchdog!" Li whines. LeMaster holds out his hand. Li drops her head and places Pepsi's leash in his hand.

LeMaster deftly removes a spiked choke collar from his back pocket, loops it around Pepsi's neck, spikes inward, and reattaches the training leash all in one liquid motion. Pepsi, overjoyed to be on the move, bounces beside LeMaster toward the center of the ring.

Arriving at the center of the ring, Pepsi does not sit. LeMaster gives a firm command, "Pepsi, down!" Consequence follows disobedience. In response to the quick, hard jerk on the choke collar, Pepsi is literally hugging the grass, his long legs spread to the four winds.

When the dog stops quivering, LeMaster says quietly, "Pepsi, sit." Pepsi slowly rises to a sitting position, sits still as a statue, his eyes glued on his commander. LeMaster takes advantage of the silence.

"Those of you who have been letting your dog get away with less than one hundred percent obedience may have to be a little rough the first time or two, but if you are consistent, your dog will catch on. It is imperative that your dog meet disciplinary consequences when he is disobedient. Never give your dog a command you do not follow through with. Expect exact obedience … every time … without exception."

"Pepsi, heel," LeMaster commands in an even tone, leading out with his left foot. Pepsi performs flawlessly for several minutes and then walks peacefully back toward his mistress. Removing the choke and replacing Pepsi's collar, LeMaster reattaches the leash and hands it back to a smiling Li.

LeMaster swaggers back to the center of the ring, smacking his fist against his palm and timing his steps to match his emphasized words. "You must *make* your dog *obey* you. When *you* walk, *he* walks. When *you* stop, he *sits*. When you say, 'Down,' he lays down until you give him another command. *No exceptions!* Anything less is not obedience."

Pivoting smartly at the center of the ring, he adds, "Those of you with large dogs on the long training leash can wrap the leash around your waist. This yields leverage against momentum." There are a few large dogs in the class: a Bouvier, a large Alsatian, an English Sheepdog, and a massive boxer. However, LeMaster is looking at Pepsi.

I had seen this trick in the training book that I had checked out of the library. The pictures revealed several advantages of the long training leash that LeMaster required for beginners because it allows long-range freedom for puppies and older dogs that are unfamiliar with the leash. Over several days, the long leash is gradually gathered in by the handler as the dog learns to respect it. Wrapped once around the handler's waist, the leverage achieves an effective, instantaneous stop (at least when the trainer outweighs the dog).

I had a chance to test this method during our early trial runs at home with Champ before we started obedience class. He quickly adopted the heel/sit position, except when he would see a cat. Once, when we were trotting along, I spotted the trouble ahead before he did. I quickly took a wrap of the long training leash around my waist, planted my feet and said, "Champ, sit!" Champ hit the end of his leash, whipped around, and returned immediately to my side, sitting squarely and looking up at me with renewed respect. Cat forgotten. Lesson learned. Was it forever?

I can only hope the maneuver will be as effective for Li as it was for me. I saw her set her jaw, square her shoulders, and wrap Pepsi's long leash around her tiny waist several times. Her waist couldn't have possibly measured more than about 15 inches, so the 20-foot leash is not appreciably shortened, otherwise LeMaster might have warned her about the potential twirling effect incurred by Pepsi's momentum. Li's father, a small man of Asian descent, added his blessing to Li's decision by bobbing his head out the window of his minivan parked at the edge of the pavement.

"*In*-side! *Ree*-verse! A-a-a-nd ... *trot*," LeMaster commands.

The Little Ones

We turn inward, toward the center of the circle, reversing our clockwise rotation. During this exercise, my attention is directed toward the lady who materializes in front of me. I'll call her Brunhilde; a broad-shouldered, well-muscled woman in a short-sleeved T-shirt who stands a good six feet tall and must weigh no less than 230 lbs. A miniature Schnauzer dangles earthward at the end of a wispy thread of a leash. The dog can't weigh even a pound.

During our walking exercise, "Scotty" trots mechanically, like a freshly wound toy. Now, with the entire class trotting, Brunhilde is less intent on Scotty than on keeping up with the class. Scotty's short little legs become a blur, like a smudged charcoal drawing.

"*Ree*-verse, *in*-side," LeMaster commands.

Handlers pivot on the right foot, dogs in tow. If the dog is paying attention, their leash will remain slack. Slackness, at his current ground speed, is impossible for little Scotty. He braces against the maneuver.

Like a water skier, Scotty strains against his little bracelet of a collar, rises in a graceful arc, maintaining his mechanical gait in midair, and lands with practiced precision. It is not due to any lack of grace in Scotty's technique that LeMaster comes to his aid.

"*Hey!* You there—with the miniature Scotty!" He storms. "*Slow down! Your dog's legs are a lot shorter than yours!*"

"I vash ondly tvyink to kip opp mit da r-r-resht off da kr-r-roop!" Brunhilde insists.

"Just … tighten your circle, please Ma'am," says LeMaster as the woman slows her pace so that Scotty can assume his trot. With a reduction in the distance per lap, the micro pooch regains a bit of dignity. Gradually, however, Brunhilde enlarges her circle again, still subconsciously trying to "kip opp."

"A-a-a-and … *halt!*" It's the command that Scotty has been working for. Instead of the expected sitting position, he flops to the ground, legs sprawled, panting in total exhaustion. LeMaster looks the other way. Did I detect a lop-sided grin?

The sitting position of Hans, the miniature dachshund whose mistress is too rotund to keep up with Brunhilde, is challenging to detect. Whether sitting or standing, Hans' leg-to-body-length ratio means that the angle of his back remains virtually unaltered. Luckily for Hans, his mistress's speed is impeded by her weight. The two women proscribing the smaller circle might have struggled against feelings of discrimination, but they really did have the inside track, as it turns out, in a later class.

Giant Steps—Not Always Progress

I peel my eyes away from Scotty and Hans and concentrate on LeMaster. He is demonstrating which foot to lead with when we break from the "sit" to "heel" position as opposed to the "sit" to "stay" position, in preparation for future off leash work. I replay the command: when I want Champ to stay (that is, to remain in a sitting position until I return for him), I am to lead with my right foot as I leave him. If I want him to rise from his sitting position and heel beside me, I am to lead with my left foot, the foot nearest him. If a trainer is consistent, the dog will know—even without a verbal command or a hand signal—just what his master desires of him.

Pepsi, galloping like a greyhound, sees absolutely no need to change direction. His training leash is a ripcord. Like a music box ballerina, Li spins like a top.

Concentrating on my feet, I am soon tangled in the long leash ... again. I almost trip myself as I try, like Brunhilde, to "kipp opp."

"Run!" shouts LeMaster suddenly. I take a couple of very short steps sideways until I can gather the extra loops of the training leash properly into my right hand. A few teams pass us, including Li and Pepsi, who are traveling at a remarkable pace.

"*Ree*-verse!" LeMaster commands suddenly. From my leash-gathering position at the outside of the ring, I see Li plant her feet and brace herself, just as LeMaster had demonstrated. Pepsi, galloping like a greyhound, sees absolutely no need to change direction. His training leash is a ripcord. Like a music box ballerina, Li spins like a top. Then Pepsi, his stride never slowing, nearly pulls Li's shoulder from the socket. Then, like a racehorse with a bit in his mouth, Pepsi runs through the center of our circle, across the park, straight toward the minivan where Li's wide-eyed father, uttering a Japanese expletive, rushes to open his side door. Bounding in great arcs behind Pepsi, Li touches down once every 10 or 12 feet, and then, with a final leap, the pair disappears into the van. Apparently thankful that his daughter is intact, the father closes the door on the obedience chapter.

When to Quit

Having observed Li's disgraceful exit, we watch for LeMaster's reaction. With a slight shaking of the head, he merely sighs, as if relieved. Intimidated by LeMaster's stern response toward the inept handlers of undisciplined canines, a couple of older ladies, right beside me, hold a silent conference and, coming to a unanimous decision, gather up their cocker spaniels and walk away into the gathering dusk.

A man with a golden lab glances at his watch. Apparently, his sum of allotted time has lapsed. He, too, decides to go. Longingly, my heart follows each of the escapees. Should I even try to continue? The words of a well-beloved poem remind me of a lesson I've quoted to Jed. What if I were to quit now?

> When things go wrong, as they sometimes will,
> When the road you're trudging seems all uphill,
> When the funds are low and the debts are high,
> And you want to smile, but you have to sigh,
> When care is pressing you down a bit,
> Rest if you must, but don't you quit.

> Life is queer with its twists and turns,
> As every one of us sometimes learns.
> And many a failure turns about
> When he might have won had he stuck it out.
> Don't give up though the pace seems slow—
> You may succeed with another blow.
>
> Often the goal is nearer than
> It seems to a faint and faltering man;
> Often the struggler has given up
> When he might have captured the victor's cup,
> And he learned too late when the night slipped down
> How close he was to the golden crown.
>
> Success is failure turned inside out,
> The silver tint in the clouds of doubt,
> And you never can tell how close you are,
> It might be near when it seems afar.
> So stick to the fight when you're hardest hit
> It's when things seem worst that you mustn't quit.
> —Edgar Guest, "Keep Going"

"We Can Do This!"

Catching my eye from his position at the edge of our circle, Jed smiles and gives me a thumbs up. I hate to disappoint him, but I'm positive I don't have what it takes to train a dog properly. According to LeMaster and the book I checked out, there will be an hour a day of repetitive exercises. Will Champ be up to the rigorous daily workouts? Will I?

Sighing, I look down at Champion. Performing flawlessly, he looks up at me with bright golden eyes full of devotion and wags the tip of his tail, nearly imperceptibly. I knew enough Champ-talk now to perceive what he meant. *"What? We can do this! No problem!"* Yes, Champ has what it takes: love, trust, and the gentle willingness to cheerfully accept his assignment. Which attribute am I lacking?

For the fourth time, I successfully loop the long training leash into my right hand. Shaking my head in frustration, I take a deep breath, lift my head, and rejoin the trainees. I will keep trying—for Jed, for Champion, and for others who might mistakenly judge me worthy of trying. What's that old saying my Grandma used to quote when my efforts didn't quite toe the mark? Oh yes—"Anything worth doing is worth doing right." Early on I picked up the lesson from responsible adults that life is a training ground of orderly steps with high stakes attached. Although we cannot earn a heavenly reward, it is a matter of choice—and obedience.

> Heaven will be cheap enough if we obtain it through suffering....
> Heaven is worth everything to us.
> We must not run any risk in this matter.
> We must take no venture here.
> We must know that our steps are ordered by the Lord.
> May God help us in the great work of overcoming.
> He has crowns for those that overcome.
> He has white robes for the righteous....
> Everyone who enters the City of God will enter it as a conqueror.
> He will not enter it as a condemned criminal, but as a son of God.
> (Ellen G. White, *Child Guidance*, p. 567)

Chapter 6

Hard Work

Rest if you must, but never say quit!

> There are thousands to tell you it cannot be done,
> There are thousands to prophesy failure,
> There are thousands to point out to you one by one,
> The dangers that wait to assail you.
>
> But just buckle in with a bit of a grin,
> Just take off your coat and go to it;
> Just start to sing as you tackle the thing
> That "cannot be done," and you'll do it.
> —Edgar A. Guest in "It Couldn't Be Done"

It's a challenge to organize our day around Champ's training walks, but they turn out to be far from drudgery. I use them as incentive for Jed to finish his schoolwork each morning. By daily repetition, Champion is soon performing well. As we go on these walks, we find evidence of people who enjoy country living—an avocado orchard, backyard gardens still producing tomatoes, and a little fruit stand on the corner where we often stop to pick up a bag of fresh oranges on our way home. It's one way to ease the pain of losing our country home.

"Will we ever live in the country again, Mom?" Jed asks.

"I know it's where you want to be, and it would surely be better for Champ," I assure him. "Your dad will not be letting that dream die. We have country in our hearts. That's why we moved to Canada before you were born."

I try not to think about losing our home. I have to sidestep that shadow every day. These obedience walks help me discipline my thoughts. It's hard work. I'm not quite as adept at focusing as is our dog.

The "Best Dog"

During our second obedience training session at Mentone Park, Champ and I are sandwiched between an energetic golden retriever, named Susie, who refuses to sit squarely, and a huge Rottweiler with a portly master whom I will refer to as Mr. R. ("R" is for Rottweiler because that is all he talks about.) While our dogs learn not to react to each other, Mr. R directs his remarks in my direction whenever LeMaster's back is turned. My German shepherd and his Rottweiler from Denmark eye one another and then growl.

With his eyes fixed on LeMaster's back, Mr. R leans toward me with a conspiratorial half-whisper, acquainting me with his dog's stellar lineage—"Herr-Von-Rotten in Denmark" (or something like that)—"out of so and so by ..." He tells me that he has been showing his black and tan wonders for over twenty years.

In the midst of his expounding on the superiority of Rottweilers, Mr. R suddenly snaps to attention. Looking up, I see that LeMaster is headed directly toward us ... toward *me!* My heart leaps into my throat! Am I going to get into trouble for listening to Mr. R? No, he passes me by to ask the golden retriever Susie's mistress if she would like some help with Susie to accomplish the coveted square sitting position.

The adrenaline rush helps me focus on the demonstration at the center of the ring, despite Mr. R's monotonous monologue. LeMaster repeatedly adjusts Susie's sitting position, but she insists on her sloppy sideways stance. I was curious as to how this habit would be overcome. I tried to listen to

LeMaster, but Mr. R was sharing Von Rotten's achievements and upcoming shows. He speaks from one side of his mouth—the side toward me.

"I have several purebreds at home besides this two-year-old, but he's the most promising champion I've ever bred. He was beribboned as 'litter champion' at six weeks and won both first place and grand champion ribbons at two other shows before he was a year old. I'm just repeating this obedience class to keep him in shape for bigger and better things."

Champion curls his lip back and growls softly at Von Rotten. The big dog returns his greeting. Mr. R jerks the leash and drones on, "We're just here reviewing for the December field trials in San Francisco. I already have the gold cup from last year's competition."

I cannot help but notice the similarities between this man and his dog. In matching black and brown, they stand together square-on, jutted jowls hanging loose, barrel-chests inhaling and exhaling in unison. It must thrill LeMaster straight through to the soles of his gleaming army boots to see such unity between man and beast! My ignorance throbs like a sore thumb, and I seriously consider relocating in some other part of the circle. As it turns out, my near proximity to Von Rotten saved my shoes.

While LeMaster tries to work wonders on Susie, the rest of the class practice the "sit-stay." This gives Mr. R the perfect opportunity for indulging in rather judgmental statements about the other teams, finally forecasting a bleak future for me in the show ring. He need not have judged me—I didn't even begin to know how much I didn't know.

What I did know was that his dog was whining very softly, as if trying to get his master's attention. Leaning against Mr. R's leg, the big dog is rebuffed with a knee to his shoulder and a sharp reprimand. The dog straightens for a few seconds and then begins to squirm uncomfortably. I think about asking Mr. R if Big Von might need to relieve himself, but Mr. R. looks about as open as a solid brick wall, and he drones on.

"Everyone should have a Rottweiler! Super-intelligent ... perfect manners ... never an accident in the show ring ... impeccable control ..." LeMaster interrupts Mr. R's dissertation with the sharp command to walk our dogs. As we move out, Big Von appears even more bowlegged than usual, and a bit ... sluggish. Unlike his usual methodical march, he has to be pulled along. The dog—champion that he was—responds obediently, head high, though with the hinder parts assuming a running squat.

"Trot your dogs!" comes the command.

The early darkness of the cloudy winter evening effectively veils Big Von's liberal deposits. Champ and I, immediately behind Big Von, can easily sidestep the generous distribution, though I am unsure how to maintain uniformity in the ranks and to warn the mistress of the Brittany spaniel behind us. Head high, intent on precision, the spaniel's mistress has pulled her dog's head slightly upward, sufficiently preventing her dog from detecting the spill ahead.

Like lemmings over the Cliffs of Dover, the remainder of the platoon, eyes fixed on the team ahead, plowed right on through. I think it was a lively red-haired Irishman with a freckle-faced boxer who finally realized what was happening and hollered an expletive. The entire class uttered a unigroan when they discovered the error of their ways. This alerted LeMaster who, with an intimidating finger, directed a clean-up command at Mr. R.

> *Like lemmings over the Cliffs of Dover, the remainder of the platoon, eyes fixed on the team ahead, plowed right on through.*

Mr. R., in spite of Big Von's impeccable record, had come prepared to scoop "Rotten leftovers." Subdued for the remainder of the evening, Mr. R. does not so much as glance in my direction. I would have been better able to control my amusement had I not peeked toward the sidelines where Jed was bent over with laughter, holding his hand over his mouth.

Sobering Threats

When LeMaster is made aware of the Rotten situation, he commands the troops to move to the court, a smooth and clean cemented area with colorful markings carefully measured out for the game of tennis.

Jed smiles as he observes shoes and paws being wiped on the grass before entering the gateway of the tennis court. He pats Champ's head, proud that he is clean. A few teams, claiming the need of a more thorough cleansing than the grass can offer, exit the ranks. It is a worthy excuse. Only two other pairs besides Champ and me escaped the Rotten disaster—those traveling in more limited dimensions, proscribing a smaller circle—Hans and Scotty. It occurred to me that a person is often better off traveling their own track, restricting themselves to a path less traveled. As we trot around the court, I sincerely appreciate the lights; the shadows had descended so gradually that most of us failed to recognize the danger at our feet.

> But if men disregard the path lighted by the heavenly beams,
> and choose a path suited to their own natural hearts,
> they will stumble on in darkness,
> not knowing where they stumble or why.
> (Ellen G. White, *Letter 16*, 1897)

As the three of us await the next phase of our training inside the tall cyclone fence surrounding the court, a low growl emerges from Champion's throat. This is out of character for our easy-going canine. The only time we've heard him growl is when he detects a belligerent dog or some sort of weapon; I have only to point my index finger at him, and he'll growl as if I have a gun in my hand. We have no idea as to the source of this defensive behavior in Champ, but we're about to receive a clue.

Looking down the darkened street, Jed and I can see the motivation of Champion's unrest—a man clad entirely in black leather swaggering in our direction. As the man arrives at our chain-link fence, we see a long, shiny machete hanging from his silver-studded belt. He glances sideways at Champion who is now barking ferociously, viciously baring his teeth, and straining against the leash in my hand. Strangely enough, it's as if no other dogs even see this man in black.

The man moves as if to unsnap the machete from his belt. Despite my protector's vicious growls, I am thankful for the fence between us.

The man looks directly at me, replaces his belligerent expression with a friendly smile, removes his hand from the handle of his weapon and swaggers away from the light of the court. Champion watches the retreating form until the man is out of sight, then glances up at me and returns to his sitting position, obviously informing me that, though he may choose to obey, protection has priority.

What seems intended to frighten me has actually settled my nerves and increased my faith. I am protected, and my heart is deeply stirred. Until this night I have been bewildered by a mysterious quotation.

> To stand in defense of truth and righteousness
> when the majority forsake us,
> to fight the battles of the Lord when champions
> are few—this will be our test.
> At this time we must gather warmth
> from the coldness of others,
> courage from their cowardice, and loyalty from their treason.
> (Ellen G. White, *Testimonies for the Church*, vol. 5, p. 136)

Though I may not see them, when the time comes to stand for the right though the heavens fall, I must remember that there are angels beside me, ready to defend and strengthen me—just as surely as they were there to guide Leta and me together so that Champion could become part of our family, neither am I alone tonight. Champion is the type; my life's journey is the anti-type. Though shadows may intervene, my Protector will not fail. Today's troubles are calculated to reinforce tomorrow's courage. After the storm comes the rainbow, seen only by those who are looking upward.

Down to the Wire

Too soon the final week is upon us. The dogs are all on regular leather leashes now. The last evening, we walk, trot, and reverse on the court until LeMaster stops us for his closing announcement. There are only about twenty teams remaining. Sitting square and silent at their master's side, each dog is quietly attentive. Sweeping his muscular arm in a horizontal arc, LeMaster indicates the details of our final exam.

"Next week your dogs will compete for honors right here in this court. You will either pass or fail. You will be required to perform off leash. Any dog who does not properly execute one of the exercises requested by the judge will fail. There will be judges and prizes awarded for proper execution of the required exercises. Those who fail will be asked to repeat the class."

Off leash! My heart is a bird in panic, thudding against my rib cage. My stomach is an elevator in free fall, disconnected from its supports. I have postponed a critical discipline, and now there is only one week left for me to accomplish Champ's off-leash training! The fact that I have never walked Champion without his leash is of no small concern. Step by step, day by day, week by week Champion has learned to obey; he comes when called, passing around behind me and sitting squarely at my left side, exactly as LeMaster requires; He heels, reverses, or stays according to voice or hand signal and has even perfected his five-minute down-stay but always with his leash attached to his collar. The right time for me to completely disconnect my connecting line with Champ has never presented itself.

We'll never be able to surmount this hurdle in a week—maybe not even in a lifetime! Like lightening before the storm, the all-too-familiar fear of failure stabs me in the gut. By the time we reach home, I am nauseous.

Of Failure, Success, and Duty

Jed is always enthusiastic as we return from our daily walks. "My Champion is the best dog in the whole class!" he remarks, plopping onto our front lawn after a particularly excellent run, Wednesday morning, December 10th, 1986. "I'll bet he gets *some* kind of a prize!" A new wave of terror seizes me, and an inaudible voice reminds me—accuses me—that accomplishment is never achieved by procrastination.

Potential failure carries with it the possibility of success in any undertaking, so why do I always come away from a challenge with such a miserable sense of dread? All week I bury symptoms of distress by munching on Tums®, but the improbability of completing our training in Master K-9 School for Dogs is very real. My conversations side-step the real issue of accomplishment.

"Jed, the real value in taking this class is not in winning or losing the upcoming competition. I didn't even know about the judges and ribbons until the announcement, but I admit that it is enticing to realize that there are a few rewards offered. The real value in the class is in teaching Champion to obey, not in acquiring accolades, right?"

He nods, though half-heartedly, not willing to release his grip on the hope that his Champion could prove to be a winner. Then he quietly puts his finger on the plague-spot in my character.

"Mom, you can do this," he says with calm conviction. "It's in your power to make Champ a winner."

What makes a winner, anyway … in the game of life? The clock of time is wound but once. What about the bigger game? It seems like I've read a poem about the one competition we play "for keeps"—the one we play against our own weaknesses. Maybe I can read something to Jed this evening about integrity, in spite of my shortcomings in obedience.

> To do your little bit of toil,
> To play life's game with head erect;
> To stoop to nothing that would soil
> Your honor or your self-respect;
> To win what gold and fame you can,
> But first of all to be a man.
>
> To know the bitter and the sweet,
> The sunshine and the days of rain;
> To meet both victory and defeat,
> Nor boast too loudly nor complain;
> To face whatever fates befall
> And be a man throughout it all.

> To seek success in honest strife,
> But not to value it so much
> That, winning it, you go through life
> Stained by dishonor's scarlet touch.
> What goal or dream you choose, pursue,
> But be a man whate'er you do!
> —Edgar A. Guest, "Duty"

During our worship hour that evening, the stark reality of the upcoming test is distracting; prize or no prize, I need to just *pass*! Tests and I have never been on friendly terms, so it has been more comfortable to avoid even thinking about the final exam. Now that knowledge has descended like a funeral pall, I dare not share with either Jed or Jere how frightened I really am. No beating around the bush—I am an amateur. That it is with a capital "A" will be as obvious tomorrow night as if I had it plastered on my back at the starting line.

Mr. R and the other professionals, just taking the class "to keep in show shape," will all be ready. But, for me, just showing up will be a major accomplishment.

Yes, we have worked hard, and we have accomplished an amazing amount of communication with Champion. Considering how little we actually knew at the beginning, where we were and how far we've come should be enough, shouldn't it?

"Even if Champ doesn't get a prize," I say, as Jed replaces the choke chain with Champ's leather collar before releasing him, "I believe he'll obey our commands. That's what I have wanted. I'm not much enthused about this upcoming test. I have just wanted him to learn. That's more important than prizes, right?" Jed shrugs and runs to his beloved dirt pile in the back yard, where he's been "digging for gold," with his Champion heeling like a pro right beside him—off-leash! I go in the house to seek the comfort of our ancient sofa.

What will tomorrow bring? Lord, it is not within my power to do what I need to do! How I use the next twenty-four hours will spell the difference between success and failure—to fail in one point, means total failure! I just can't take that leash off and make a practice run—it might not be perfect, and I need to be perfect! Champion might not obey me. He might run away. He might get hit by a car ... like Tramp.

Too Late to Hope?

I feel the fear climbing upward through my body. Beginning with my "cold feet," it has now taken possession of my leg bones. I recognize and dread the advancement of the sensation. It's the same feeling of dread I used to get when taking final exams in high school—fear that was strong enough to make me fail questions to which I knew the answers. It's the same feeling that accompanies my spiritual battles when failure appears imminent. Surely procrastination, putting off the gaining of a spiritual victory, is not important enough to be included in a spiritual category ... is it?

> To defer work which needs immediate attention until
> a more convenient time is a mistake and results in loss.
> The work of repairing sometimes amounts to double
> what it would had it received attention in season.
> Many fearful losses and fatal accidents have occurred by
> putting off matters which should have
> received immediate attention.
> The season for action is spent in hesitancy,
> thinking that tomorrow will do;
> but tomorrow is frequently found to be too late.
> (Ellen G. White, *Testimonies for the Church*, vol. 4, pp. 452, 453)

Am I too late to hope? Participants in LeMaster's obedience class have dwindled steadily until it is composed almost entirely of show-experienced purebreds, those who were already on short leashes the very first night. And, of all those dogs in perfect attendance, Von Rotten is a shoo-in for first place.

I wouldn't want to appear covetous, but I do wonder, just a little bit, what that first-place ribbon looks like. I wonder if Mr. R. might let me touch it—that is, if we were to actually show up for the final exam? But there will be no reason to attend unless I am able to accept and overcome the challenge. Remember Edgar Guest's dare?

> But just buckle in with a bit of a grin,
> Just take off your coat and go to it;
> Just start to sing as you tackle the thing
> That "cannot be done," and you'll do it.
> —Edgar A. Guest, "It Couldn't Be Done"

Big Von's accident forcibly demonstrated to me that there is a proper time and place to avoid an "issue." My reaction comes easily, an automatic and proper side-step. However, there comes a time when I must meet a messy problem head-on, and I must surrender my fear to reason. I must not only come up with a plan but execute it—immediately—with expertise, as if I possess the skill I need. Procrastination leaves no space to circumnavigate the challenge that is dumped on me just because I think I might fail. Sometimes I just have to get my hands (or feet) dirty by committing to getting the job done.

My work has been right under my nose for several days, but I wasn't willing to look at it. Now I have but one day to accomplish the impossible. I have to be strong enough and dedicated enough to solve the mystery of "teaching Champ the last trick." I must "buckle in with a bit of a grin," as if I have a Helper who believes that, together, we can accomplish the impossible.

Deciding that a job must be done, accepting His timing for its accomplishment, and then humbling myself to admit and accept help is the hardest part of the work. My work is to create the perfect crisis, make sure Champion accepts the bait, and then avert his reaction—all in less than five seconds. It sounds impossible. A good share of my comfort comes through the assurance that others have passed this way before and learned the last trick successfully. But I wonder if it isn't just plain too late to try.

Chapter 7

The Last Trick

The most important lesson is learned in the last mile.

> Courage was never designed for show;
> It isn't a thing that can come and go;
> It's written in victory and defeat
> And every trial a man may meet.
> It's part of his hours, his days and his years,
> Back of his smiles and behind his tears.
> Courage is more than a daring deed;
> It's the breath of life in a strong man's creed.
> —Edgar A. Guest in "Courage"

Elusive Target

In my dreams I am desperately trying to "kipp opp," as Brunhilde would say, but I can only walk in slow motion. Choke chains, leashes, judges, and awards are tangled in a plethora of color and noise. When I awaken, my burden of hopelessness is heavier than the one I took to bed. If only I could turn back the clock, perhaps I would try a little harder to accomplish the required task—*before* the last day.

The off-leash assignment has been evasive; like a semester project that's not due for several weeks, my effort has been inefficient. With the passage of time, the requirement has increased adversely to the number of days available. The statistical probability of solving my dilemma is approaching zero. The appearance of that all-important "distraction" and its immaculate timing is highly unlikely. Only an angel can arrange it for me now.

The same all-encompassing feelings of dread and fear that engulfed me during finals week in high school and college have wadded themselves into golf ball sized rocks bouncing in my stomach. Tonight, dog and master must be a perfect team; Champion must obey me by hand signals or voice only. Already I am beginning to feel like a used Kleenex® poised over a garbage can. Nothing short of divine intervention will find us fully prepared for our "Court" appearance and the judge's verdict! The golf balls in my stomach have stopped bouncing and have turned to lead, impeding me from getting up.

I am too sick to take our walk today, I reason. I must prepare Jed for failure.

The Fog Moves In

"Rest if you must, but don't you quit!" The words of poet Edgar Guest are as clear in my mind as if he had spoken them right beside my bed as I struggle to an upright position. What I must do and what I am capable of doing are totally incongruous, but opposition to my self-proclaimed inability is bound to be even more brutal. Short of death itself, I suspect that neither Jere nor Jed will give me permission to back down from my appointed task.

Even though Jere has not been to the training class, I know where he will stand regarding tonight's performance even before he comes home from the lab. He has taught Jed to face up to life's challenges: broken toys are either fixed or thrown out, none of this willy-nilly sentimentalism. There are a few homeschool classes that Jed doesn't like; reading, spelling, and writing are challenges that I tend to side-step. If my little boy tells me that his eyes hurt, that he has a "reading headache," or that the sunshine is calling and he can't possibly stay in the house any longer to read even one page, I believe him. Jere doesn't—he calls it "fog." My inability to detect fog is legendary. Jere is amazed that I can so readily succumb to Jed's excuses. With minor variations, Jere and I have repeatedly had the same conversation.

"Where's Jed's spelling list for today?" Jere will ask as soon as he arrives home from work.

"Uh … he said he can't remember any of the words we studied yesterday," I shrug. "Besides, he bumped his head, remember? And, it was so *nice* outside today."

"Fogged again, eh, Linda?" Jere will frown, shaking his head as he clucks his tongue once against the side of his cheek in exasperation with my inconsistency. When he reduces my comfortably gray smudge, my *dots of defense*, into distinct tones of black and white, I can clearly see that the dynamics between teacher and pupil are not exactly what they should be. Jere believes in him enough that Jed gets the job done.

Why can't I see that at the time or do that properly, I wonder? Maybe it's because I want homeschool to be fun. Even the things Jed doesn't want to know should look inviting—entertaining even. Shouldn't they? Discipline makes school too much like work. I realize that the exact lesson that Jed needs—even in character building—is too often being side-stepped when I can't bust his fog. I do try, or at least I promise myself, to do better. However, at the first sign of resistance, my tightly coiled resolve dissolves like ropes of sand. Implementing Jere's technique looks impossible.

Hmm … Master K-9 class is not unlike homeschool, is it? Am I in danger of being like—like Mrs. Poodle—just appearing good, and not actually accomplishing the necessary work? Obedience school should be a prerequisite for parenthood! I want Champ to be able to perform properly in his class the same way I want Jed to learn spelling and reading, but the discipline is … is just too difficult! Those off-leash commands loom like a mountain to crush me! I just don't possess enough skill to accomplish total obedience—not for boys or dogs, either one—do I?

Time to Walk the Walk

At breakfast, my stomach refuses to digest even half a banana. I'm thinking about how to apply the last few pages of the instruction book and paying closer attention to my choice of leading with my right or left foot while directing Champion. If I lead with my left foot, he heels. If I lead with my right, he stays. It's reasonable, and yet my feet seem to forget which to use when I'm surrounded by dogs and people ... and judges ... soon. I can't seem to still that voice in my head that keeps insisting that perfection is unreasonable.

Jed hurries through his lessons—even spelling and reading. He quickly stashes his schoolbooks and grabs Champ's training collar and new leather leash. Surely there must be something else for me to do. My son and his best friend wait together patiently on the front lawn for the most important activity of their day. It will be an absolute miracle if I don't disappoint them both.

"C'mon, Mom!" Jed calls to me. "Time to teach Champion the last trick! Have you got the 'tosser'?"

I nod mutely. Curiosity and fear wrestle like porcupines fighting over the wad of petrified fruit in my stomach. *Can* Champion do this? Can *I*? Jed's enthusiasm trumps my fear ... for the moment.

Hopscotch Rescue

According to both Dan LeMaster and William Kohler, off-leash perfection hinges entirely upon precise application of the "throw chain." The description of this small but indispensable instrument is like the "tossers," or markers, with which I armed myself during the epic hopscotch battles in elementary school.

Hopscotch began in ancient Britain during the early Roman Empire. The original hopscotch courts were over 100 feet long and used for military training exercises. Roman foot-soldiers ran the course in full armor and field packs to improve their footwork, in much the same way that modern football players run through rows of truck tires today. Roman children drew their own smaller courts in imitation of their soldier fathers, added a scoring system and a marker, which was usually a common stone.

> *Curiosity and fear wrestle like porcupines fighting over the wad of petrified fruit in my stomach.* **Can Champion do this? Can I?**

The English term "hopscotch" comes from "hop," which means "to jump," and "escocher," a French term meaning "to cut." To "scotch" a rumor means to scratch it out, and "butterscotch" is a hard candy that is made in large sheets and then "scotched," or cut, into small pieces. To "scotch" in the game of hopscotch means that your turn is finished by missing the mark through either stepping on a line or misjudging your toss. Modern hopscotch courts are often painted on school grounds but are no doubt the most common artwork chalked onto sidewalks around the world.

For passionate love of that game, my best fourth-grade friend, Susan, and I became "tosser connoisseurs." We experimented with shaped and taped chunks of newspaper; we tested key chains, wooden pucks, tangled nails, even a couple of nifty necklaces that Susan confiscated from her mother's jewelry collection. Tossers had to be just right—not too heavy, not too light. Shape was critical, with no uncollected tails hanging out. They had to have enough weight and be of the right smoothness to slide when they hit the pavement, yet small enough to nestle precisely onto the last numbers, at the far end of our chalk pattern, without touching a line. We often finished a game at recess without touching a line with our foot or our tosser.

After some weeks of scientific evaluation, Susan and I mutually concluded that metal was the material of choice, that weight was a critical factor, and yet that there had to be a certain amount of "give" to the design—it must be able to slide smoothly into correct position, without bouncing or screeching to a premature stop. If we had recorded our time-consuming and complicated research into scientific terminology, Susan and I might have earned a TPhD (Doctor of Tossology).

Calling upon that most important fourth-grade achievement, I perfected the instrument designed to teach our Champion the last trick—our *magnum opus*. Actually, I was inspired weeks ago, during one of our first walks, to stop at the local hardware store where I stroked different gauges of chain displayed on spools against the back wall. Wadding experimental lengths of chain, I tested them for weight and texture, finally purchasing a length of medium weight, chrome-coated links that I twisted into a small, lightly knotted figure-eight.

According to our Kohler book, properly applying the element of surprise will redirect a dog's attention from any distraction back to his handler (without the usual tug on his collar to remind him who is in control). I am to inconspicuously disconnect the leash from Champ's collar (leaving the leash in its usual position in my hands). Champ is to practice his usual commands—heel, sit, down, stay, by my hand signals and body language alone, never knowing that he is disconnected from the leash. Mr. Kohler also mentions that obedience is most needed during emergencies. Yet, as with a child, obedience must be secured *before* you need it! The object of the leash is to bring the dog past any point of contention against it. Today we teach Champion that distractions are his cue to pay even closer attention to a command. Rereading the chapter, I realize that I should have brought a couple of extra "tossers," in case I fail to connect properly on my first try or I am unable to properly accomplish the element of surprise.

The book makes it sound simple, and yet, as I play the scenario in my mind, I doubt I can accomplish the exactitude this maneuver requires: (1) Don't let your dog see you throw the chain or hear the tiniest sound from your pocket, (2) Don't miss the dog, (3) Don't let him see you pick up the chain.

Like a secret nuclear test, I have practiced with my tosser until I know how it will perform. I grip it like a lifeline in my pocket as I step into unknown territory. Swallowing hard and then taking a deep breath, I send up a prayer for help. Our walking routine is familiar. By now, Champ's level of obedience should no longer depend on his physical attachment to me. However, this has to be proven by a test—a distraction or temptation worthy of pursuit. At the golden moment, when Champion is tempted to sacrifice obedience for thrill of pursuit, the tosser will come into play. The key to success, it seems, is in timing, secrecy, and one-hundred-percent accuracy.

Contact!

We venture onto the back streets of Mentone. I again touch the silver wad of chain in my pocket. I can feel my lack of faith being replaced by my fourth-grade fervor for the game. I stop. Champ automatically sits. I stealthily unclip his leash while giving him a hug. When I ask him to heel, he sticks to my left side like glue—walking, trotting, running, sitting, and staying without a word of command. He ignores several occurrences that might have caused other dogs to lose their focus, but we have to wait for the right one. We walk nearly half an hour off-leash with Jed keeping a sharp eye for the cat that he is sure will provide the distraction we so desperately need.

"I don't see one C-A-T this morning, Jed."

"We'll find one, Mom. We'll walk until we do!"

Suddenly there she is! A perfectly unsuspecting feline at the prescribed distance. Champ's ears focus like twin radar receivers. It's time!

I stop. Champ stops beside me, but he does not sit as usual. He is not obeying. His eyes are on the cat. Careful not to let the chain rattle, my hand slowly closes around the silver wad in my pocket.

"Don't panic, Mom," Jed whispers, "and only use the chain if he starts to run."

"Champ, sit!" I sternly command. Champ sits down, his gaze still on the cat. Will the cat distraction overrule his respect for my authority? He makes his decision. The instant he leaps away from me, a miniature version of that familiar old hopscotch pattern superimposes itself on his rump. Almost without a conscious thought on my part, my well-engineered tosser finds its mark. Champ jerks his head around to identify his "attacker." I do not need to repeat the command. The cat is forgotten. Champ returns to my left side, assumes the sitting position, and looks up at me expectantly. By leading with my left foot, I silently "ask" him to heel while Jed secretly retrieves the wondrous wad of chain on the pavement behind us. Champ obeys me perfectly all the way home, without a leash, without a voice of command. We end the walk with his five-minute down-stay. It's precision incarnate.

Have we experienced divine intervention, an unseen hand guiding our efforts in providing the "purr-fect" distraction and helping me hit the target? There is no doubt in my mind that Champion is ready for tonight's test. Am I?

As Jed removes Champ's training collar, gratefulness wells up in my heart. My butterflies have landed. The lead golf balls are gone. Lunch tastes good.

Attempt at Bribery

I try to remain encouraged after the morning's successful off-leash run, but as the sun begins its descent, my mouth is permanently dry—no matter how much water I drink. My head aches. Eating supper is out of the question. My stomach is so full of butterflies again that they hardly have room to flutter, but none of the boys in my home will acknowledge even the remotest possibility of my imminent demise. Chewing on a couple of Tums®, I kneel beside Champion, seeking the "warm fuzzies" I always find in his brindle fur.

"Champ, I'm so scared!" I say, enveloping his shoulders in a desperate hug as I pour my woes into his ear.

He turns his majestic head toward me as if to say, "What's there to be afraid of! Everything's under control."

"I can't *do* this!"

How can I expect a mere dog to ever understand the importance of human ... pride—is that what I am feeling?

"You seem to know your lines, Champ, but I can't count on my brain not blanking out under the pressure! I know I'll fail! I will lead with the wrong foot; I just know it!" I close my eyes. In the stillness it occurs to me that there is one more tool that I am not above indulging—bribery.

"Champion, if we pass tonight, I'll get you a nice big, juicy steak on the way home!" He cocks his ears, wondering if he has heard correctly. Meat and bones are a rare treat in this veggie house.

Fever of the Moment

The next thing I know, Jere is looming above me, arms folded across his chest, not unlike LeMaster himself. Leaning forward, he pats my head as he would a frightened puppy, pulls me up from where I have collapsed on the floor, and gives me a quick hug.

"Come on in and eat something before you go," he says.

I shake my head and suck on Tums® and drink more water while my men eat their supper. I am sweating—profusely. Why—I'm burning up! Mamma used to excuse me from PE classes for less fever than this! I stumble to the living room and collapse on the couch. Though I try desperately to ignore them, it's too late to deny myself the indulgence of tears to coat one last excuse.

"I have a fever." Jere and Jed look at each other. They nod and grin at each other conspiratorially. They don't even answer me.

"Come on, Honey," Jere consoles, when he has put away the leftovers. "You'll do fine! You've been working hard with Champ every day. I'm sure he's learned his lessons. I don't think you have a thing to worry about." His words are intended to bring me comfort, but he is incapable of fully appreciating, or even *beginning* to understand, the impossibility of my situation. He has no idea what I am up against. He hasn't been to dog-training court. Who knows what those judges will look like? Not only am I up against the "best of breed" champions, I am up against fear itself! I will fail … in front of everyone! I hold my head in my hands and press on my eyes in a vain attempt to plug my tear ducts. My heart, swinging like a lead pendulum, bangs against my rib cage.

Tick-tock … yes-no … win-lose … stay-go … tick-tock … yes-no … win-lose … stay-go ….

"Don't panic, Mom!" Jed gently squeezes my arm. He enjoys repeating this recently acquired philosophy: "Champ knows his stuff."

"I'm not worried … about Champ!" I gasp, trying to control my tendency to hyperventilate. "It's *me* that will fail!"

"Could this be fog?" Jed's dimples deepen as he leans in close and looks into my eyes. "Just remember the *rules*. It's *easy*. Isn't that what you tell me about spelling and reading?" I shut my eyes and slowly shake my head. School has absolutely no bearing on my illness … does it? I manage a lop-sided grin and nod slightly.

Jere pulls me up from the couch and gives me a hug, a bit too firmly. I gag on a hiccup. How can they have finished eating so quickly? I need more time … more Tums®. Jed grabs Champ's training collar and leash. Three dignified males are looking expectantly at me. I rise to my feet.

"You coming?" I ask in a squeaky voice. Jere shakes his head. He is taking a class in immunology to update his microbiology licensure as well as working full time. This crisis is entirely of my own creation, anyway. Begging his support would reduce me to mere sentimentalism. My attendance should come from my sense of integrity … finishing the job I started six weeks ago.

As I rummage through my purse hoping not to find my keys, some words from Howard Walter's well-known hymn tend to cool my fevered brain.

> I would be true, for there are those who trust me;
> I would be pure, for there are those who care;
> I would be strong, for there is much to suffer;
> I would be brave, for there is much to dare.

Though the words are written for a much higher calling than finishing a dog obedience class, I realize anew that integrity affects every aspect of life. I *must* be true, even though I know I don't have what it takes to be perfect. It's time to practice faith—as small as the proverbial mustard seed. It's not the first time I have experienced the shadow that can stifle my pitiful efforts at bravery, and it won't be the last. Who knows, with another dose of divine intervention, maybe my own feeble effort will get me through the terrors of even this night. I turn the knob and step into the future.

> It is you that determines your fate,
> You stand with your hand on the knob
> Of life's doorway today,
> Success asks you to say
> Just what you will make of your job.
> —Edgar A. Guest, "The Job," adapted

Chapter 8

True Blue

Just showing up is half the stress of the victor's cup!

> Life's battles don't always go
> To the stronger and faster man;
> But soon or late the man who wins,
> Is the one who thinks he can.
> —Walter D. Wintle in "Thinking"

Call to Arms

Driving to the park I contemplate the execution ... the final exam ... the last exercise. It will be a judge's assignment—probably some combination of a figure eight, a reverse, a stop and sit with a five-minute down-stay, and then the command for our dog to come to his handler from a distance—all off leash. Champion's accomplishments cannot be faulted. On the other hand, there is his handler who still, on occasion, leads with the wrong foot after giving him the command to stay. Fondling the comforting collection of Tums® in my skirt pocket, I begin to wonder if I brought enough to keep my butterflies sedated.

The trip from our house to Mentone Park is far too short. When we arrive, parking is at a premium. From a distance Jed and I can see that a large crowd has gathered near the tennis court. Desperately fingering the remaining Tums® in my skirt pocket, I approach the mob, Champion in tow. So many people! Where are the dogs?

Very few dogs have been able to persuade their owners to show up for final exam, but of those that have come, it appears that entire families—apparently even distant relatives and mere acquaintances—have turned out in droves to watch the final performance. Of those who have made the effort, one darling little blonde cocker spaniel is disqualified because she is in heat.

"Too distracting for the males trying to concentrate on their commands," rules the head judge. I read both disappointment and relief in her owner's sigh as they disappear into the deepening twilight of the comfortably cool winter evening. This leaves thirteen dogs to face the gauntlet.

The remaining dogs appear to be purebreds—show dogs—practicing for stiffer competition. Champ has no proof of his lineage, but he is not intimidated. Head held high, ears erect, he sits attentively, a fine representative of his German shepherd heritage. My weak hands are strengthened by his calm confidence.

Only LeMaster is absent. Taking his place are three professional judges. The head judge asks us to line up on the foul line in the court. I notice that my hands leave sweat marks on Champ's new leather leash. I pop a couple of Tums®. They turn to powder in my dry mouth. I choke. Champ looks up questioningly. I swallow hard, wishing I had remembered to bring water.

The head judge monotones her instructions. Her hands glide like mechanical ballerinas through the air in exaggerated precision, motioning like an airline stewardess pointing to the exit doors in case of disaster.

"You will begin with 200 points. You will lose points for errors in performance—errors committed by either you or your dog. You will first be asked to walk your dog ... on leash ... around the court. ..." Her final words morph my last handful of Tums® into a large, suffocating clump in my throat.

"Unless your dog passes *every* test, on and off leash, you will be asked to *repeat* the class."

I look at Champ. He glances up at me, mouth shut and eyes bright, wagging the tip of his tail ever so slightly as if to reassure me, "We're ready!"

I take a deep breath and blow it out very slowly, through puffed cheeks. I still don't feel ready, but the time has arrived.

The Battlefield

There are seven pairs of dogs and handlers on the near side of the court with Judge One, and six pairs on the far side with Judge Two. In the far court, I can see that Mr. R and Von Rotten are looking smart, dressed to match, as usual, in black and tan. I fumble desperately in my pocket for one last vestige of comfort while repeating to myself, "Tum-ta-tum-tum-

> *I still don't feel ready, but the time has arrived.*

tummmm. Drum roll for the death march. Tum supply kaput!" Thankfully, I'm not expected to speak; my tongue is stuck to the roof of my mouth.

Judge One's instructions are lost to me, so I follow the group for our first exercise, starting off on my right foot, the wrong foot. Oops, imperfect execution of the first command! I had thought: *The left foot is the right foot ... right? Nope; right is right.* Out of the corner of my eye, I see the judge make a mark. Is it against me?

Don't panic! Hey, maybe I should adopt Jed's favorite saying tonight—don't panic; don't panic.

Heel ... walk ... reverse ... trot ... stop ... sit down ... stay. Champ performs flawlessly, his leash remaining slack regardless of our speed. After what seems like an eternity of performing and waiting for others to perform, it is time for the "five-minute down-stay." Champ has always done well in practice, but, with the final moments of court in session, the atmosphere is supercharged. Every dog is restless, confused by the stress. Champion still appears calm and composed despite the mounting terror that must be pulsing down through the leash from my sweaty palm.

We walk our dogs to the far side of the court and then give the "down-stay" command. Champion drops elegantly and squarely. I remove his leash and walk back the full length of the court without him. I feel his golden eyes boring into my back as I return to the foul line and turn to face him. Sure enough, he is looking at me intently, loyally awaiting my command.

Was there ever such a long five minutes? It hurts to breathe. Lest Champion misread a false move, I must remain motionless. Though I try not to move my hand, the clip on my empty leash rattles. While I try in vain to invent saliva, I sense a slight movement at the far foul line. Curiosity overcomes my dedication to discipline—I risk glancing away from Champ.

A little Pekingese with a bright pink bow gathering her mop of normally unruly bangs decides she's been without her beloved mistress long enough. Bouncing gaily across the court, she is gathered up by her mortified handler. They are immediately swallowed by the gathering gloom.

Disobedience can give the appearance of devotion.

Champ glances at Pinky for a particle of a second and then back at me. Within seconds, a beagle sitting next to Pinky decides that he's had enough, too. Then a boxer near Champ is bit by the bug and returns to his owner. Then the toy collie returns, then a golden lab, until, by the end of the required time, only eight dogs remain bonded to the pavement. Von Rotten is, of course, among these dedicated finalists.

At the end of the five-minute infinity, Judge One signals for us to break the "down stay" by returning to our dog. Each team is then asked to "finish with a flourish." One set at a time, we are to perform—off leash—a crisp figure 8, reverse right and reverse left (combination of inside and outside turns) at a brisk trot in a tight circle. Then each handler is to stop abruptly with our dog sitting squarely beside us. We are to perform these feats as the judge calls out the commands. Impossible! I feel faint. Several teams have performed before an idea comes to me.

Just as we are called to center court some words form in my head, "Walk a little faster than usual." Champ tends to travel a step ahead of me on leash (which is a fault), so I establish a brisk pace for our first command in the off-leash exercise. Champion and I melt into precision. The commands come in a clipped tone, easily understood, and, before I can realize, we are done—our moment in the spotlight is at an end.

I reattach Champ's leash and return to the foul line where the teams from the far court join us eight abreast—the remnant. Von Rotten and Mr. R appear beside us, smug and silent, chins up. I take a deep breath and lift my chin, too—pretending that I belong—and I await—with bated breath—the judge's verdict.

This scene reminds me of the great Judgment Day when I will be judged in the heavenly court, not by lineage, conformation, color, or rank ... but whether I have obeyed the Judge's commandments.

> Here is the patience of the saints:
> here are they that keep the commandments of God,
> and the faith of Jesus.
> (Revelation 14:12)

The Prize

After a quick conference, the chief judge removes several beautiful ribbons from a large, transparent plastic bag. There's a white one, a purple one, a red one. Last of all, out comes a huge blue rosette with streamers that look at least two feet long, embossed in gold—the first-place ribbon! The evening breeze glorifies the prize as the judge waves it aloft. I sense a trickle of saliva. Is my mouth watering because of covetousness?

Another judge drapes the ribbons across her arm and falls into line behind the chief judge. They walk toward the remaining survivors, preparing to distribute the awards for bravery above and beyond the call of duty. The fourth-place winner receives his ribbon. The third-place winner leaps into the air with enthusiasm. Von Rotten and Mr. R receive the red ribbon for second place.

The judge then stops in front of Champion, royal blue streamers waving gloriously in the evening breeze. As if in a dream, the ribbon is floating toward ... me

Suddenly the whole world is clapping—even the judges! I am numb. Mr. R is the first to reach for my free hand.

"Well done!" he says, pumping my hand vigorously. Champ and Von Rot touch noses. They know better than to growl ... now. They are graduates ... now. They have both finished "in the ribbons!"

I look around at the sea of faces. Such a cloud of witnesses! I search for Jed, but tears blur my vision. I merely wave the ribbon in his direction, knowing he is watching. Wiping the mist from my eyes with the back of my beribboned hand, I look up just in time to catch a glimpse of someone who looks like—Dan LeMaster? There, at the back of the crowd ... no, he is smiling. Can't be him. Can it? I wave the ribbon in his direction. The man waves back, gives me a smart salute, and disappears into the night.

Hands reach out to congratulate me as I make my way toward Jed. My smile is genuine. No more "pasted countenances" for me! I float to Jed and drop Champ's leash at his feet.

"You did it, Mom! You did it!" Jed grins, hitting me with a high-five, and then envelopes his Champion in a big hug. "I knew you could do it!" Then, as if peering into my heart, he says, "Your stomach is better, too, right?"

I rub my abdomen. It's true! "Hmmm, must be an enchanted ribbon!" We laugh. For a while today, I wondered if I'd ever laugh again. It feels so good!

I trace the blue rosette with my finger. What a blessing I might have missed had I decided not to try tonight! What if my men had allowed my fear to shackle me? The ribbon is not just for Champion's flawless performance, but it is also to remind me to work faithfully each day toward the only prize worth having.

As we walk to the car, I recall another starry night, barely three months earlier, when Heaven descended through clouds of doubt and darkness to assist me with Champion's adoption. By the time I reach the car, I am convinced that Heaven has helped us again.

Taking Champ's velvety head in my hands before he jumps into the back seat I say, "Thanks, Champ, for everything!"

"Read me the gold part, Mom!" Jed asks, holding the ribbon toward me as I start the car. The message glitters, reflecting the streetlight outside.

"Master K-9 Obedience Graduation First Prize."

"Read me the certificate, too!" he insists just before I pull out into the stream of traffic.

"Master K-9 School for Dogs—Diploma of Graduation. This is to certify that Champion, a male shepherd mix, owned by Jed Franklin, has completed a class in novice obedience training and is hereby awarded this certificate of accomplishment. Dated, December 11, 1986. Signed, Judge Randi Guerro: Instructor, Dan LeMaster."

"Champ really *is* the best, isn't he Mom?" Jed's dimple deepened. "My champion!"

"Yes, he is!" I assure him. "And I'm going to get your Champion what I promised him I would if he were good tonight!" Jed is all smiles as he inspects his treasures up to the moment. I pull into the Winn-Dixie parking lot.

"Wait here with your Champion," I say to Jed. I feel confident leaving Jed in Champ's care. Walking into the store, I recall a session during our second obedience class when Champ had begun growling during a demonstration carried out by a uniformed officer and his huge black Bouvier from the San Bernardino Police K-9 unit. Didn't he like the Bouvier? When I focused down the block to where Champ was looking, I could see a man who was heavily tattooed and smoking a wilted cigarette swaggering closer. He was dressed in black and was swinging a night stick. Champ strained at his leash. Only when the man was out of our range of vision did Champion stop growling and straining at his leash. I knew, then, that Champion had a strong protective instinct. With confidence I left Jed in Champion's care while I bought the steak.

Standing By

When we reach home, I present the slab to Champ in the front yard. Halfway back to the porch I remember that he is still wearing his choke collar, and I recalled LeMaster's warning, "Never leave a choke collar on your dog except during training exercises!"

"Oh Jed, I forgot to remove his choke collar!" I say, dropping the bag of bloody steak wrappings on the lawn. "I'll be right back." Champ growls as I reach toward him. (This was the only time in his life he ever growled at me, except when I looked into his eyes and pointed my finger like a gun, which was his signal to sound and look vicious.) Rather than risk a misunderstanding at the end of such a wonderful night, I retreat back to the porch.

"Where's Champ's choke collar, Mom?" Jed asks, reaching for the doorknob.

I avoid looking directly at Jed. "Well, um, he growled at me," I say.

Jed frowns, first at me, then at Champ. He hands me Champ's ribbon, graduation certificate, and report card, then resolutely stalks toward the wild beast devouring the mound of bloody flesh in our front yard. What does a mother do when she trusts her son and trusts his dog but senses a crisis brewing between them? I cover my eyes, leaving a finger's width of space for peeking. Jed leans down, mutters one word in a soft, slow, gradually descending tone, implying his great shame and displeasure.

"Cha-a-a-amp!" Jed intones with supreme disapproval.

Champion stops eating, swallows hard, licks his chops, and looks up expectantly at the boy he loves (even more than steak?) and patiently waits while Jed pulls off his choke collar.

"Having trouble recognizing dog-fog, again, Mom?" Jed asks, jangling the collar in front me. The porch light glitters on the chain. It deepens Jed's dimple and makes his blonde hair shine. I give him a quick hug, accidentally banging the metal choke collar against the front door.

"Thanks Jed," I say in deep humility. "Thanks for helping your Champion obey. And thanks for helping your mother see through the fog!" Jere opens the front door in response to the chain clattering against the door. Jed shows him the big blue ribbon.

Jere lets out a long wolf whistle, "Did *everyone* get a ribbon like that tonight?"

"Nope!" Jed smiles up at his father, "Just Champ, Dad! He won first place! Three other dogs got second, third, and fourth place ribbons, but most of them went home with nothing."

"Well, I guess he really *is* a champion!" Jere said, watching Champion wolf down his steak. "What's he eating?"

"The steak Mom promised to give him if he passed obedience class!" Jere laughed in spite of what he might consider a needless expenditure on our tight budget.

"Just think, Jed!" I say, "If we … I … hadn't persevered, Champ would have missed his treat!"

"Oh, yum!" Jed says, pinching his little vegetarian nose in mock repulsion. "What a scrumptious incentive!" We all laugh. It's a family portrait that lingers on the canvas of my heart: the three Franklins gathered in the circle of porch light. The most valuable, however, are the ones that I hold deep within my mind and soul, indestructible illustrations that will forever remind me of one of the most amazing experiences of my entire life. Despite my lack of faith, what a wonderful day this has been, perfect in every way—once I surrendered my weakness to His strength.

I exchange the choke collar for the leather one with Champ's ID tags, drop the steak wrappings in the garbage can, and walk back toward the front yard. Alone for the first time since I arose from my bed with dread in my heart, I close my eyes and breathe out a prayer of sincere thankfulness. Without divine aid, I doubt that I would be able to feel the comfort of the evening breeze. I would not be able to sense the nearness of the angels standing by, ready to help this poor mortal (Zechariah 3:5, 7; 4:14; Hebrews 1:14).

Champion is still gnawing on his steak bone. Head high and shoulders square, I approach Champion with the knowledge of having an angel beside me. Surely an angel has been helping me all day; the same angel who was with me in Leta's living room the night she gave Champ to me, likely the same angel who smiled at my mother's angel in the delivery room the day I was born.

Confident in the unseen, I replace Champ's leather collar without incident and lift my eyes to the night sky to behold the glory of the night.

Yes, my son, never doubt that there are angels standing by.

We had no inkling of how much we would need Champion in the immediate days ahead. Given the choice, Champion would have happily sacrificed his ribbon if he could have prevented the catastrophe that was about to befall his beloved master. Our son would soon need the loyal devotion of a faithful friend in the long, dark valley just around the bend in the road of his young life. It was a valley so thick with mists and shadows that I would become unaware of the light behind, the angel beside, and the rainbows above. Thankfully, Champion was there, as a spectacular reminder of God's love, care, and provision—even before we called upon Him. We lost so much in the fire, but, amazingly, that big blue ribbon did not burn!

And it shall come to pass, that before they call, I will answer;
and while they are yet speaking, I will hear.
(Isaiah 65:24)

All our sufferings and sorrows, all our temptations and trials,
all our sadness and griefs, all our persecutions and privations,
and in short all things, work together for our good....
All experiences and circumstances are God's workmen
whereby good is brought to us.
Let us look at the light behind the cloud.
(Ellen G. White, *My Life Today*, p. 185)

Chapter 9

"Please Don't Die!"

The desperate plea of a little boy is heard.

What if this year has given
Grief that some year must bring,
What if it hurt your joyous youth,
Crippled your laughter's wing?

Only your heart can pity
Now, where it laughed and passed,
Now you can bend to comfort men,
One with them all at last.

You shall have back your laughter,
You shall have back your song,
Only the world is your brother now,
Only your soul is strong!
—Margaret Widdemer in "To Youth After Pain"

After the Storm

Shortly after Champion's successful graduation from obedience school in Mentone, our family relocated to a remote cabin located in a high valley in the foothills of the San Bernardino Mountains. Within three days of settling into our cabin, an accident occurred that left us physically and emotionally in a dense cloud of smoke and ash—one that left Jed's life hanging in the balance with Jere and I groping blindly through a maze of gloomy shadows that only those who have endured injury by fire can fully comprehend.*

[*Our family's journey through fire, the medical details, emotional trauma, our move back to Jed's hometown in British Columbia, and the answer to Jed's doubts that anyone could love him in spite of his severe scarring are more completely described in the first book of this series entitled, *Rainbow in the Flames*. Because of editing restrictions, Champion's role in Jed's healing was not included in that account. Yet, he was there, and he was taking up the slack with ropes that would have been otherwise too short to accomplish Jed's full-scale rescue.]

Such rugged mountains and dark valleys we would never have voluntarily attempted to climb. Good friends helped us, quite literally, pick up the singed pieces of life. There were two things that Jed asked about when he could speak. The first was: "How's Champ?" Champion was staying with friends, but they brought him to the hospital to see Jed—once through the window when he was first out of ICU and once to have a picnic on the hospital lawn.

Jed's next question was, "When can we move back to Canada?" Neither Jere nor I knew about the possibilities of moving anywhere— especially Canada. Jed was still in Intensive Care.

Jed's Prayer Answered

We were, miraculously, invited to return to our home in British Columbia, mere hours after Jed made his wishes to return to Canada known. Jere and Jed were overjoyed. I wasn't sure but that a move might just introduce more unnecessary change into our already overwhelming new world of therapeutic requirements. I was so thankful for Jed's spared life, but each new day seemed to bring new medical challenges. Did Canada even possess modern technology in burn injury recovery? Thankfully, my fears for Jed's continuation of medical care were ungrounded. We discovered that the burn unit at Vancouver General Hospital was very advanced.

Jed's one constant, ever-glistening bow of promise in his trial by fire was Champion's unchanging dedication. Time after time, Jed had seen Champ adapt to whatever adjustments life tossed in his direction; he would calmly consider his surroundings and then, very consistently, make the most of them. When Champ's original family was unable to keep him, he joyfully accepted his new assignment with Jed. Despite having to adapt to the blazing heat of a southern California summer, this amazing animal added nothing but pleasure to our lives. He aced his difficult obedience assignment, lending a little of his courage to me along the way. After the fire, he stayed with friends until Canada emerged as a possibility. Did he whine and fuss over the temporary separation? No! Again, he adapted, but his level of joy knew no bounds when we retrieved him from our caring friends.

As soon as we were able to transfer Jed's medical records to Canada, we pulled up our California stakes and headed north. Jere had instant employment at the college as soon as we arrived, so, while I tried to organize the kitchen, build beds, and put the office in order, Jed and Champion went exploring together those first few days after our return to the ranch.

Time with Champion in the great outdoors was the motivating factor for Jed to finish his homeschool classes each morning. As soon as the last "t" was crossed, out came the bike and away went the boy with his dog in the lead. It was often on roads he'd never traveled before—bumpy country roads that camouflaged exciting encounters with tuneful birds, saucy squirrels, sleek deer, yipping coyotes, evasive wolves, fleet-footed rabbits, and sometimes even a stubborn moose or belligerent black bear.

When Jed was first discharged, some of his wounds were still leaking. His weakened muscle tone after six weeks of hospitalization caused him to desire rest, and his scars may have encouraged social distancing. But he did not let these "minor difficulties" keep him indoors—even while Champ was unable to join us in our apartment across the street from the hospital. Without his knowing, I watched from the window of our apartment and winced when he fell from his bike. I tried not to overreact, but my heart was breaking as I gently tended the torn scar on a freshly bloodied knee.

Fortunately, Champion introduced a superior plan early in Jed's healing process, one with a much more effective long-range goal that did not include mushy motherly platitudes.

The Dog and His Boy

Only near-blizzard conditions or an occasional illness could interfere with Champ and Jed's Canadian explorations. Nearly every day after Jed's homeschool assignments were finished, they would play outside for a while in spite of the cold. It wasn't long before I realized that Champion was teaching Jed lessons that I could not: how to let his spirit soar against the winds of adversity, like a kite rising ever higher against a headwind. Champ taught him enthusiasm, how to value his moments in the sun and how to take time to watch the clouds—in short, how to catch rainbows.

Only near-blizzard conditions or an occasional illness could interfere with Champ and Jed's Canadian explorations.

I watched in wonder as Jed rose to heights he would not have known but for the captivating combination of his three-way education: the physical and emotional demands of healing, books and lessons that included spiritual allegories, and the unwavering devotion of his optimistic dog. The blessings and challenges were comfortably intermingled. I saw progress in Jed's level of interest in life, his disposition as well as his character. Is it only in the dark times that strength of character is formed—the same qualities I could see in Champion? I listed a few.

- accepting
- adaptable
- brave
- cheerful
- companionable
- devoted
- discerning
- energetic
- enthusiastic
- gentle
- honest
- loyal
- obedient
- optimistic
- outdoor loving
- patient
- protective
- respectful
- truthful
- tranquil
- unselfish

Champ's devotion and encouragement were powerful influences for strengthening Jed's character, like bookends, holding him upright. Their unwavering joy and acceptance of the two were complimentary to each other. Ease and relaxation do not create a winner; it is the exertion that results in the overcoming of obstacles that makes a person strong, bestowing upon him the demeanor of a champion in proportion to the effort expended.

Often when my heart was hurting over the scars that Jed would bear the rest of his life because of a few seconds spent in the flames, I would see a rainbow. Fortunately, Champion took up the slack left by my inability to rise above my regrets. From the very beginning, he taught Jed to focus on the rainbows, not the rain. Who can deny that storm clouds, blessed by sunshine, increase the possibility of rainbows?

There were times Jed needed parental guidance, but there were more times when he needed unconditional acceptance without words, times that could only be satisfied by a good friend who believed wholeheartedly that today was the best day in the history of the entire world. As Jed began taking the extra-long strides required of a burn survivor, Champion was that friend. He didn't allow Jed to wallow in self-pity; there were mountains to climb and rainbows to watch.

Numerous scientific studies have proved that dogs have the ability to lower stress by stimulating chemicals in the body that lower both blood pressure and heart rate. Although I never measured the physical effects of Champion's presence, the dog and his boy seemed to assume that any day was improved when they were together.

"Mom, I have ten reasons to cry," Jed said to me one day when I was being particularly regretful of his injury, "but I have a hundred reasons to be happy! And so do you!" In a blur of legs, dog and boy leap out the door to see what's new down on the Sukunka shoreline. I chuckle, finally remembering where I'd left my smile; Jed had it in his pocket, again.

Returning from a hospital visit, we were caught in a blizzard. It took us a day to cover the distance that usually took a couple of hours. I strained and fussed about the snow, especially when a semi left us in a whiteout.

"Jed, I can't even see the traffic lights behind me, how can he see so far ahead? Just look at this snow!"

"Mom, don't look at the snow," Jed said, painfully raising his head. "Look at the road. You can still see the line. That's all you need to know."

Excluding weather challenges, the trips home from Vancouver are usually more enjoyable than the trips in a southerly direction. Painful surgeries and therapies, the realities of permanent scarring diminish in the excitement of returning to our sanctuary.

Nothing lifts Jed's spirits more than splashing in the creek, or skipping rocks in the river, and exploring woodland trails with his remarkably versatile dog. Champion always meets him in the driveway whenever we return home, even for a short trip to town … except once.

Missing Dog

This day, after we've been away from the ranch just a few hours, our beautiful German shepherd is not at home to welcome us when we arrive. We call for him and search everywhere we can think he might possibly be, all without success. We phone our neighbors. No one has seen Champ.

Finally, with a sense of foreboding, I dial the number of a man I'll call "Mr. Q," who raises turkeys and pigs. He has threatened to shoot Champ if he ever comes near his stock or flock. His daughter answers the phone.

"Yeah, Champ was here today," she says. "My Dad shot him. He limped away."

My heart turns to ice. Is our beloved Champion ... dead? or at least badly injured? Is he holed up somewhere slowly bleeding to death? Surely he would have already returned home if he were able. It's getting close to sundown! Where would Champion try to hide his pain from the boy who has had too much already? In vain we search for a couple of hours.

Desperate plea

"Jed, we'd better pray," I say, kneeling on the living room floor when we return home for a drink of water, rest, and, hopefully, some inspiration.

"We've been praying and calling all afternoon, Mom," he protests, nevertheless he falls to his knees and opens his heart one more time. "Dear Jesus, please show us where Champy is. Amen."

Suddenly, a clear picture flashes into my mind: a door, an injured dog lying on the floor inside. I recognize the door. "We have to look in the old schoolhouse, Jed."

"But Mom, we already went by there and called him."

"All I know is that we need to go back there," I insist. "This time we must open the door."

I don't visit the old school building except when necessity demands; the large structure is not one of my favorite places. It was once our worship and training center, the hub around which our school activities revolved. Upon our return to Canada, I had swept it out and put it in order, but painful memories continued to lurk there, memories of happier times—Jed's growing up years before we were asked to leave, before the fire mountain touched us. That was another lifetime. With an enormous sense of foreboding, I slowly push open the door and peek inside.

There, in a pool of blood, is our Champion. His eyes are glazed, his mouth is dry. He does not lift his head or wag his ever-expressive tail.

"Oh Champ!" I say, pressing my ear to his chest. His heartbeat is slow, but he's alive.

In our absence, he had wandered away from home and into trouble. In an effort to find a place of safety, he had jumped through the hole where the glass had fallen out of a narrow window opening. Weakened by loss of blood, he was unable to jump back through the opening or even answer our earlier summons.

"Champ!" Jed cries out. "Oh, Champy, please don't die!"

I run home for the car. Jed stays with Champ. Together, we load him into the back seat and speed to the veterinarian clinic where a few pellets are removed from his shoulder and hindquarters.

"These don't contain lead," the veterinarian says, squinting at a bloody piece of metal. "Weak as Champ is right now, I don't advise surgery to remove whatever pellets might be remaining inside of him. Take him home. Convince him that he's got something to live for."

> *"Dear Jesus, help Champy get well soon. Please don't let him die until I'm all growed up. Amen."*

Back home we tempt Champ with his favorite treat—pancakes and peanut butter. We shower him with compliments, saying what we've always believed but didn't tell him. We tell him how much we love him, that he is a gift from God, and that we need him to stay with us for as long as possible. At worship hour, we discuss how bad things can be turned to good when we are willing to learn from them, and then Jed prays a simple closing prayer.

"Dear Jesus, help Champy get well soon. Please don't let him die until I'm all growed up. Amen."

Their role reversal only increased their mutual love and respect. It wasn't long before they were back on the trail. I taught Champion to heel. He taught Jed how to heal. Which was the greater accomplishment, I wonder?

Together

Alone was not in the description
Of what I was sent here to do.
I am here to help in your healing,
I'm so happy to be here with you.
No action or play is too rigid,
No trail or mountain too high.
Through sunny or shadowy weather,
We'll teach each other to fly.

Keeping up with Jed after he got his quad was more demanding, but Champ was always game. Wherever Jed wanted to explore, Champion would scout ahead, flushing out dangerous critters like grouse, squirrels, deer ... and, every once in a while, a bear or two.

The best time of any day was when Jed could just be a regular boy—doing chores, riding his quad, collecting wood, gardening or exploring—any time he could be outside with his dog.

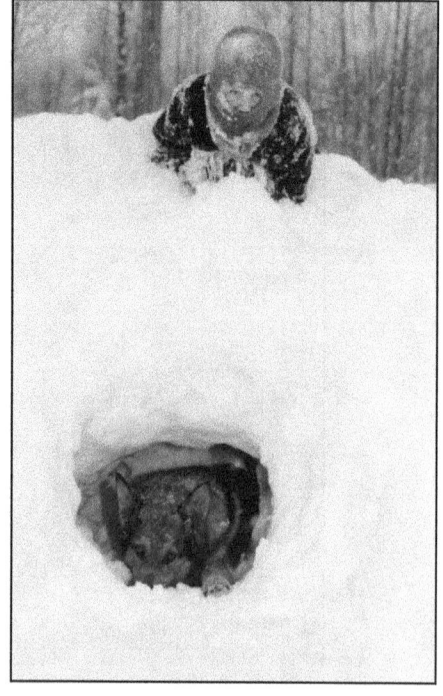

Rain or shine, sleet or snow, Champ was always ready to go.

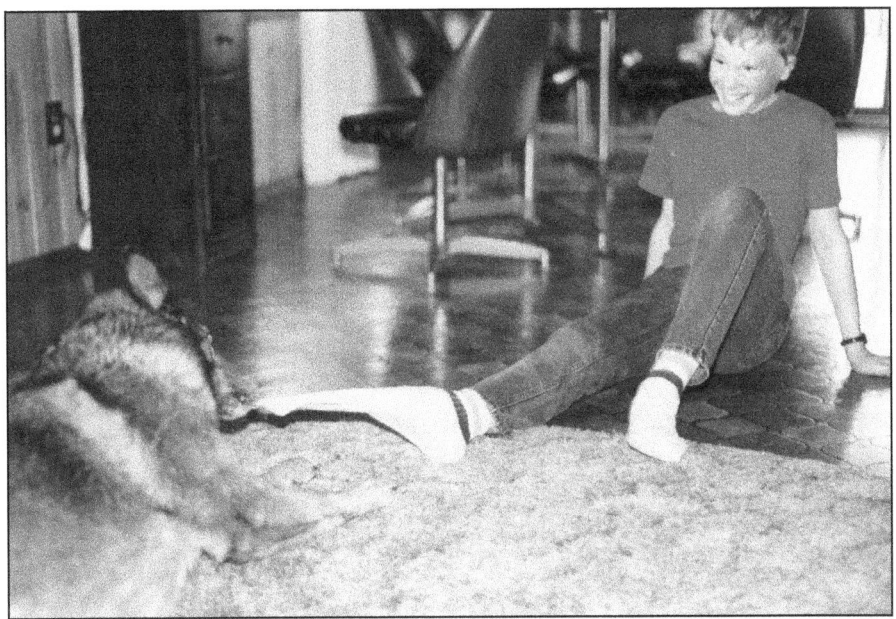

Togetherness didn't stop just because Champ and Jed might need to stay indoors for a few hours.

Schoolmaster

After two incidents in obedience class when he detected weapons (a nightstick and a machete), Champ never again appeared aggressive ... with one notable exception. The mother of a five-year-old visitor had repeatedly asked him not to keep pestering Champion. The boy was blowing in Champ's ears, pulling his tail, and bouncing on him. After patiently enduring this mistreatment, Champ raised his head, looked the child in the eye, lifted his lip and emitted a warning growl.

"Leave that dog alone!" commanded the boy's mother for the third time.

Champion endured a few more seconds, but his seemingly endless patience was at an end. He finally growled viciously, bared his teeth and lunged at the boy's face. Although I had never seen Champion bite anyone, I was fairly certain that there had to have been some serious damage inflicted to the boy's face. I sat immobilized.

"Mommy, Mommy!" yelled the boy holding his face and running for the safety of his mother's arms. "He *bit* me!"

"Show me the blood," his mother calmly replied, unconcerned.

The boy swiped his hands across his nose and inspected them for blood. His hollering subsided as he grinned sheepishly up at his mother. There wasn't a scratch on the boy anywhere! Champion had only impacted the boy's face with his own nose, leaving a non-physical, but extremely effective impression on the mischievous little boy.

Among his other intelligent attributes, Champion was a great teacher. Jed learned to trust his warning growls whenever they ventured on new turf. More than once, Champ left no doubt in Jed's mind that he would sooner lay down his life than allow harm to come to his boy.

Somewhere in the process of weaving in and out among the shadows of pain and the sunshine spirit of his faithful dog, the gift of empathy was bestowed upon our son.

'Tis pity not to have a dog,
For at the long day's end
The man or boy will know the joy
Of welcome from a friend.
And whether he be rich or poor
Or much or little bring,
The dog will mark his step and bark
As if he were a king.

Though gossips whisper now and then
Of faults they plainly see,
And some may sneer, from year to year
My dog stays true to me.
He's glad to follow where I go,
And though I win or fail
His love for me he'll let me see,
By wagging of his tail.

Now if I were to list the friends
Of mine in smiles and tears
Who through and through are staunch and true
And constant down the years,
In spite of all my many faults
Which critics catalog
Deserving blame, I'd have to name
My ever-faithful dog.

'Tis a pity not to have a dog,
Whatever be his breed,
For dogs possess a faithfulness
Which humans sadly need.
And whether skies are blue or gray
Good luck or ill attend
Man's toil by day, a dog will stay
His ever-constant friend.
—Edgar A. Guest, "A Dog"

Chapter 10

Happy Trails

Enjoyable memories don't just happen;
we must create them.

Some day the world will need a man
of courage in a time of doubt,
And somewhere, as a little boy,
that future hero plays about.
Within some humble home, do doubt,
that instrument of greater things
Now climbs upon his father's knee
or to his mother's garments clings.
And when shall come to him that
call for him to render service that is fine,
He that shall do God's mission here
may be your little boy or mine.

Some day the world will need a man!
I stand beside his cot at night,
And wonder if I'm teaching him,
as best I can, to know the right.
I am the father of a boy—
his life is mine to make or mar—
And he no better can become than
what my daily teachings are;

> There will be need for someone great—
> I dare not falter from the line—
> The man that is to serve the world
> may be that little boy of mine.
> —Edgar A. Guest in "The Man to Be"

The Need of Friends

Early in his life, Jed recognized his need of friends. He was only four years old when he asked about the trip to British Columbia that Jere and I had taken with some associates shortly after we'd first met each other.

"Was I there when you and Daddy went to Sundburg Ranch?"

"No, Jed. That was before we were married. Daddy and I were just good friends back then."

I was not prepared for his reaction; his little chin started to quiver, and he got tears in his eyes.

"But ... but I ... I ..." He was trying hard to express an intense feeling, "I *wanted* t' *be* there!"

I suppressed a giggle and gave him a tender hug.

"It was on that trip that Daddy and I came to realize two concepts that shaped our future; first, we were becoming best friends, and, secondly, we decided that British Columbia would be a nice place to live."

"Well ... when will *I* have a best friend?" he asked, "one that I can laugh with and make memories with—so I can remember when I am *old*—like you and Daddy?"

I smiled, again, at Jed's concept of my advanced age, but he wasn't trying to be funny. He wanted me to know that he placed a high value on camaraderie, joy, and the intricacies of forming long-term relationships.

"Happiness is a gift we give ourselves by choosing friends who value our ideals," I assured him. "A good friend is an encouragement during the tough times in life. I am thankful you recognize the value of having good friends."

As he matured, Jed became a discerner of character. He enjoyed associating with boys his age, but, for the most part, he was careful not to be negatively influenced. As a young teen, I overheard him say to a group of friends, "Why do kids feel like they have to rebel against their parents? I *like* my parents!"

Wheeling into Adulthood

As I squint back down the passage of time, I can clearly distinguish influences that played a critical role in the formation of Jed's character. It was not just the obviously important happenings that shaped his moral fiber but also those things that seemed almost insignificant at the time: casual acquaintances, disciplinary consequences, maintaining a schedule, the reading of uplifting stories, useful labor, and quiet times all played significant roles in his maturity.

Then, too, it seems like metallic threads have been genetically woven through the minds of boys. Given the opportunity, the love of all things that can be pushed, ridden, or dragged on wheels seems inborn and intensifies with the passage of time to a life-long interest in the world of machines. The downside is that these metallic filaments can magnetize them toward taking unreasonable chances unless tempered with caution and common sense.

Long before Jed could talk, he ran his assorted car collection with loose lips and guttural throat noises before he heard any other boy make those sounds. His first usable vehicle was a red wagon. With his wagon and his first dog, Tramp, he spent many happy hours collecting treasures from the forest surrounding our remote cabin in the wilderness. Jed preferred the out-of-doors, as close to nature as possible. His dad and his dog were his best friends. He certainly never suffered from nature-deficit disorder, an illness found among city children that causes them to lose focus on reality. Although it may not have appeared that he was learning, he contemplated and closely inspected his surroundings; he removed bark, compared the structure of different leaves, and listened to the birds. He fashioned roads with rock borders in the dirt with his Tonka trucks. While his dad and his dog were his best friends during those formative years, Jed was also enraptured by anything that had gears or wheels; content to be pulling, riding, and eventually driving a vehicle—*any* vehicle.

Jed graduated from play to work when Jere made him a wheelbarrow from scrap lumber, a pair of old lawn mower wheels, and some leftover paint. He loved hauling small split wood for my cook stove and then, as his muscles developed, he gradually added bigger logs for our wood heater. It was from this hand-made vehicle that Jed learned an unforgettable lesson in responsibility when his cherished wheelbarrow became kindling after he left it parked behind a pick-up truck.

Why mention Jed's wagon and wheelbarrow? Simply because playing or working, life, as Jed saw it, revolved around wheels. The fact cannot be ignored—wheels definitely have to do with the making of a man. Vehicles are a form of identity: they develop common sense and a good work ethic, teach mechanical skills, and come with a generous scoop of responsibility. Wheels and motors would eventually play a significant role in Jed's formation of friendships.

After becoming intimately acquainted with the mechanics of trikes and bikes and able to make his own repairs, Jed fell in love with a contraption that someone had constructed around an old tractor seat, a lawnmower engine, and metal pipes. Though I can't recall the particulars of how it came to belong to Jed, he and Jere spent many happy hours tinkering on "The Oddyssey" (definitely spelled with a double "d"). It was an exciting combination of gadgetry, noise, and speed, but it would never have passed a safety inspection! I was fearful of the exposed pulleys and was extremely relieved when someone bought it and hauled it away.

Snow Machines

The only way to really enjoy life in the north country is to learn to appreciate winter. Referring back to the days when sled dogs helped navigate this great expanse of land, the old-timers tell us that northern Canada consists of two seasons: six months of winter and six months of poor sledding!

Fortunately, Jed loved every activity associated with winter—cross-country skiing, sledding, ice-skating, and tunneling in the snow to play hide and seek with Champ (photos in chapter 11). It was only natural that he would gravitate to snow machines.

Though it would be a few years before we actually purchased a snowmobile of our own, Jed and Jere stumbled across a deal that was just "too good to resist" and found themselves reconditioning a "dead" Sno-Cat. This large contraption had tracks that were three feet wide and, according to the seller, would "climb a nearly-vertical wall through pure powder." The Ford inline six-cylinder engine needed some maintenance, and the rear-end required several repairs, but, after several weeks of work and then a few hours of testing it in deep snow, Jere and Jed finally calculated that the reason the machine was overheating was due to the undersized radiator.

With certain modifications to accommodate the new radiator, the machine ran smoothly. A local oil field supervisor spotted the old machine, which held good memories for him. He drove away with the old Sno-Cat on his trailer and a big smile on his face. Jere and Jed realized a little income and a whole lot of quality educational time.

Early Adventures

It was springtime when we moved back to Canada. Champion had not learned to respect the power of a northern river, swollen with melting snow. As we hiked above the Sukunka in late May, Champion was rapidly swept downstream when he stepped into the water. The bank was steeply undercut, so he could not get out of the river. I ran ahead to a lower place along the bank where I grabbed his collar as he rushed past me. It was a close call. Jed's look of gratitude and a safe dog were reward equal to the risk.

Later that summer, we were enjoying Sukunka Falls when I heard a loud gasping sound above the noise of the falls. When I attempted to locate the sound, I saw Champion bobbing among the floating logs and sticks, unable to get a foothold back to shore. By the time I noticed him, his energy was spent, and his nose was barely above the water. The rock beside him rose steeply above the pool in which he was trapped. I was able to hop down toward him. With the last of his energy and his eyes riveted on mine, and while blowing a spray of water each time he exhaled, he finally made his way to the foot of the rock. When he was close enough, I reached out, grabbed his collar, and dragged him up the side of the rock where he was finally able to scramble up on top and collapse in exhaustion. I stayed with him until his energy returned, and we both dried off a little.

After these two close calls in the river (plus one situation when the ice was unsafe and he fell into shallow water), Champion recognized a force untamable and stayed along the shore. He did not fear to cross the river on the gondola erected by the Canadian environmental team who test the river intermittently. Champ's birthright left a deficit in the swimming department, but he did become a seasoned water warrior.

> *When I attempted to locate the sound, I saw Champion bobbing among the floating logs and sticks, unable to get a foothold back to shore.*

Jed enjoyed renewing his friendship with boys he'd grown up with until age five when we left Canada. Among these friends was a boy named Trevor, just his age. As youngsters and early teens, Jed and Trevor spent a significant amount of time accumulating stories that they still laugh about today. Trevor and Jed were born three weeks apart. His mother and I had worked at the Chetwynd hospital during our early years in the north. I was a lab tech, and she was an x-ray technician. She and I shared many common bonds; we attended the same church and loved animals and creativity in many forms. (For Jed's wedding, she created a stunning multi-tiered wedding cake, while I fashioned fresh cut flower arrangements, boutonnières, and hand-held bouquets for the bride and her sisters.) It was only natural that our sons would grow into their wheels together.

Learning to operate a snowmobile is a worthwhile skill, considering the number of snowy months in our little corner of the world. Jed was as enthused about Trevor's friendship as he was about the machine that Trevor shared with him one wintery day. Trevor seemed oblivious to Jed's scars. He only saw what they had in common. They shared many adventures in the years to come and are still friends today.

Jed's childhood friend, Trevor (left), let's Jed (right) test-drive his new snowmobile. Champion (background) never demonstrated jealousy over any of Jed's friends.

First Quad

When Jed purchased his first quad, he chose a Honda 125. With it, he and Champion clocked in many hours on the numerous game trails, right-of-ways, and dirt roads of our beautiful valley. They ran more than one bear up a tree and surprised coyotes, deer, elk, and moose.

Jed's only serious injury on any of his four-wheelers happened while racing his 125 in the gravel pit to the south of us. He came home a little later than I expected. He was walking, and his faithful Champion was at his side.

"Oh, I didn't hear you drive in!" I said when he arrived. When I turned around, I saw that he was cradling his right arm.

"Are you *hurt?*"

"Yeah," he sighed softly. "My thumb got caught under the throttle lever when I flipped on a side hill in the gravel pit."

"You had a *wreck?*"

Jere walks over to drive Jed's four-wheeler back home while I grab the car keys and head toward the hospital where I know my good friend Penny, Trevor's mother, will be on duty. As soon as the x-ray is dry, she lets Jed see the picture.

"Yes, your thumb looks broken, Jed."

In the emergency room, the doctor tells us that setting the type of break Jed has suffered will require the skill of the orthopedist at the QE2 (Queen Elizabeth II) Hospital in Grande Prairie. Jed spends a wakeful night at home, an uncomfortable three-hour journey to Alberta, and then a long wait in the Grande Prairie ER before being seen by the specialist. If only the waiting could have prepared us for the intensely painful setting of that bone!

I have to hold Jed's arm in such a way as to brace against the physician's "fine-tuned adjustment,"—actually, it appears to be a *mighty* jerk without benefit of the anesthetic being fully engaged! Assuring himself, via x-ray, that Jed's bone is in proper position, the orthopedist puts the injured hand in a cast and sends us home. We are physically and emotionally exhausted yet hungry enough to eat our first meal of the day before leaving the city.

As we leave the city, the sky is ablaze with a sunset that appears more magnificent than either Jed or I can recall having seen before. Survival can do that—make the mundane seem marvelous when the crisis is past!

Whatever the cause, the sun is setting in a blaze of glory, covering us entirely with a canopy of purple and gold as we head west.

Jed takes a deep, but shaky breath, sighs softly, leans back, and surrenders his pain to the splendor of the evening. We remain silent until the afterglow has faded into deep night shades.

I sense that Jed has something to say. Because he wore a mask for three years, I learned to read nearly expressionless nuances. I wait silently until he has edited the thought.

"A sunset wouldn't be as beautiful without clouds, would it, Mom?" His wan smile touches my heart. "It's the clouds that catch the color."

Jed values metaphor, similes, and parables. I have used them often in his homeschool classes. I nod and smile knowingly. Hurting hearts need not explain a mutual epiphany. On otherwise gloomy horizons, the eye, opened by suffering, detects a magnificence in the landscape of life that was not there before the suffering was endured. To this day, the glow of that moment warms my heart.

Adventurous Friends

In their late teens, Trevor had an XR-400 dirt bike, while Jed's machine of choice was a racing quad, a Honda 400 EX. One summer afternoon, Jed and Trevor had been riding in the gravel pit when they got the idea to ride across the ford in the Sukunka River and explore the right-of-way toward Hassler Flats. Right of ways in the foothills of the Rocky Mountains where we live are often just a calf-path through the bush. Even to experienced riders these wilderness by-ways can be challenging.

"I don't know, Jed," I hedged. "Is it safe? You'll be traveling too far and too fast for Champion to go with you, and Dad and I much prefer your safety." They mistook my indecisive commentary as permission.

They packed light—as light as anyone could possibly pack—taking nothing with them except their helmets as they rushed out the door.

"We'll be back in just a couple of hours, Mom," Jed assured me with a wave of his hand as they departed in a cloud of dust.

But they didn't come back. It was almost nightfall before the phone finally rang. Jed's weary voice comforted my fears. "Can you come and get us please, Mom?"

"Where *are* you, Jed?" I tried to muffle my decibel level with gentleness, but I had been conjuring up the worst injuries and situations possible for three hours. Worry intensified my tone, "Are you *hurt*?"

"No, we're OK. Just tired," he answered. "We're at Peggy's." Peggy was Trevor's second cousin. She lived more than thirty miles from us on the Hart Highway in the direction of Prince George. I would get the details later.

"I'm on my way! It'll take me about half an hour to get there." Jere was busy at home, so I hopped in our pickup and headed out to Hassler. Penny had already picked up Trevor before I arrived at Peggy's house. It was late enough that I dispensed with visitation but thanked Peggy profusely for being there for our boys.

The expedition turned out to be a spur-of-the-minute decision that helped Jed and Trev learn how to better estimate time, distance, fuel consumption, stamina, and safety. By the time they concluded their error in estimating the mileage, they were nearer to Hassler than home, had consumed over half of their fuel, and were approaching physical exhaustion. They decided to attempt to reach some form of civilization by nightfall so as not to encounter the grizzly whose tracks had added speed and adrenalin to their adventure. They had no way of contacting civilization. (This adventure happened long before cell phones were available, and there is still no cell reception in that stretch of wilderness!)

There are times when stony silence will sink a lesson deeper than a reprimand. It seemed to me that the lights of home and his usual Champion hug held more significance for Jed that night.

> My son, hear the instruction of thy father,
> and forsake not the law of thy mother.
> (Proverbs 1:8)

Freefall

The summer Trevor acquired his first quad, a Kawasaki Bayou, he invited Jed to come riding with a new friend of his. (I'll call her Meghan.) This time, Trevor knew the variables of the gritty landscape ... or so he thought. When Jed arrived, Megan enthusiastically hopped on behind Trevor, and Jed followed them to the gravel pit not far from Trevor's house, a landscape of ups and downs equal to any amusement park. Trevor quickly climbed the highest peak, one that he thought would make for a lively descent, maybe even coax a squeal from Meghan.

As Jed watched from behind, Trevor passed the point of no return and disappeared from sight. There was a descending yell ... and then ... dead silence.

Jed raced over to discover what he feared might be true. Someone had removed a truckload of gravel from the backside of "Trevor's Mountain." Trevor and Megan were in a silent heap at the base of the ten-foot drop, with Trevor's four-wheeler on top of them! The wheels were still spinning when Jed arrived.

"Trev!" Jed yelled. "Are ya OK?" He hopped off his four-wheeler, quickly removed his helmet, and bent over the injured riders. They were groaning, so Jed knew they were both conscious, but he could see that things were not OK. When they nose-dived, the quad had turned in the air just enough to land on its front-end, still with enough momentum to flip forward and fall on top of them. Jed pulled off the quad and helped them to their feet.

Dazed, Meghan gingerly felt of her arms and legs, back and head. "I, uh, think I'm all right," she said spitting out some gravel and pulling her hair out of her eyes. "I banged my head pretty hard on ... on something ... what happened, anyway?" she asked with a frown.

When Trevor stood up, he grimaced and held his right arm aloft. No words were needed—it was obvious that it was broken. His hand hung in such a way as to give his wounded appendage the appearance of an ostrich's neck. He had put his arm out in front of him as he descended, presumably to break his fall.

"What should we do, Trev?" asked Jed.

"Hmm ... well ... I can't drive, but it looks like my quad might be drivable ... Meghan can you take the quad home? I'll ride home behind Jed." The three of them made it home without further incident. Trevor's mother, Penny, could see without taking an x-ray that her son would soon be in a cast. Trevor revealed the details of the accident as Penny drove Trevor and Meghan to the hospital. It was Sunday, and Penny was on call. When she heard how the accident happened, she reiterated to Trevor how dangerous it was to take a rider on his quad.

This would not be the last time Penny would x-ray her adventurous son. Neither was it the last time Jed and Trevor would help each other out of life's close calls, but they did become safety-conscious young men who eventually joined our local search and rescue squad. Experience is a good teacher, a hard taskmaster, and it tells the most thrilling stories for the benefit of posterity.

> A friend loveth at all times,
> and a brother is born for adversity.
> (Proverbs 17:17)

The Lord knew the value of such adventures and asked the children of Israel to repeat to their posterity the thrilling accounts of their escape from Egypt, the crossing of the Red Sea, and their other numerous deliverances. Mutual recollections of their deliverance from close calls become joyful stories worth retelling to upcoming generations. No video game can compete with the reality of knowing God's protection first-hand.

Jed was learning the value of human friendship; a friend picks up the pieces without belittling a bad decision. Unlike a dog, however, a true friend will remind you about a poor decision if he sees you setting yourself up to make the same mistake again!

Call to Restoration

Jed eagerly counted down the days until he could have a driver's license. His plan was to use the money he'd saved from his summer job mowing the golf course to buy the truck he would drive for his test the day he turned sixteen. All the trucks that he and Jere looked at fell short of measuring up to Jed's research until they found a fleet vehicle from a local lumber company—a '77 Ford F-250 4×4. I refrained from comment, but Jed saw the question in my expression. "It'll be really great when I get done with it, Mom!" Jed reassured me. "You'll see."

Jed saw his truck as it could be and would be—painted and trimmed, lifted and torqued, re-shod with new mud tires and sparkling rims, with a shiny new 460 engine modified with performance parts and a customized drive train, including drive shaft, transfer case, a heavy-duty clutch, and Dana 60 differentials in both front and rear positions, a Warn winch, an aluminum bed liner with matching tool box, and a protective moose bumper. His friend Charlie, a local mechanic, taught Jed how to accomplish a few installations where he had questions, and I upholstered the interior with black faux bearskin fur.

Jed's truck held the reputation of being the toughest truck in town.

"It's just as I pictured it would look, Mom," Jed nodded on the day he took us for a ride. Champion, head and tail held high, looked as if the bed had always belonged to him. I could actually see my reflection in the shiny green paint. I think that was the day I sensed that restoration was more than a hobby, now—it was becoming Jed's calling card. Previously he had rebuilt a few broken toys that I thought were beyond repair, fixed wrecked bicycles, and even reconditioned a couple of toasters and a tape recorder. Whenever we approached civilization, I frequented secondhand stores to obtain small appliances in an economical attempt to satisfy his quest for mechanical knowledge. So many times in his childhood I stumbled onto a dismembered home fixture spread around him in orderly disarray.

"… just to see how it works, Mom," he would say with a grin on his face and a screwdriver in his hand. "I'll put it back together." And he always did—even as he did to the last nut and bolt on his new truck—in perfect working order.

There was a friendly rivalry among the 4×4 enthusiasts in Jed's circle of acquaintances. "Now I can pull any Chevy in town out of the mud holes at Sundance Burn, Wrecking Bar, or Graveyard Creek!" Jed commented with a mischievous grin.

We're still using Jed's truck, though it bears some scars from hauling building supplies, agricultural amendments, and countless loads of firewood from our surrounding forests.

As the years have passed, Jed has expressed regret about the time and money he spent on his "tough truck," hoping that his example will not be a source of encouragement to other young men to feed their pride. God sometimes overrules our foolhardiness, though there are often consequences to pay. Working on his truck was a useful employment, possibly even a giant step toward Jed's conversion. Just as Jed viewed his truck unfinished but potentially useful, so God saw *him* as being merely unfinished but useful with the proper repairs to his character. God was patiently waiting to see the reflection of His image in the heart of a young mechanic.

The Call of the Wild

Although Champ enjoyed riding in the bed of Jed's truck, his favorite activity was still hiking the endless network of woodland trails with his best friend Jed. As far as Champion was concerned, nothing could equal awakening to the freshness of a morning in the heart of nature beside his master. The peaceful Wapiti Valley, where Jed and his dad built a wilderness cabin together, was a preferred location for absorbing soul silence.

It was in the quiet times, watching a stream and listening to the birds, that Jed contemplated his future. With one hand caressing Champ's head, he asked himself the important questions that every young man must ask as he sees his teen years diminishing: *How should I spend my life? What is my work for God? Will I be able to find that special someone who can help me with that work? When will God reveal His plan?*

> When every other voice is hushed,
> and in quietness we wait before Him,
> the silence of the soul makes more distinct the voice of God.
> He bids us, "Be still, and know that I am God."
> (Ellen G. White, *The Ministry of Healing*, p. 58)

While he awaited guidance, Jed attempted to surrender his desires by claiming one special verse in Psalms, interpreting it to mean that God would impart to him the correct desires of heart if he put the Lord first.

> Delight thyself also in the LORD;
> and he shall give thee the desires of thine heart.
> (Psalm 37:4)

The sequencing of the response to Jed's questions were as important as the answers themselves. Jed became irrevocably convicted of three things: (1) He was to grow food—the end times require it. (2) He would be shown his mate while he was doing the work God asked of him. (3) He would not have to go on a soul-mate search, for she would come to him.

By doing what Jed knew he should do and by listening to nature's voice, he was directed to know God's will for his life. (For explicit details of this development in Jed's life, read "Love Tap," a story of divine intervention in *Climbing the Heights,* the third book of the *On a Wing and a Prayer* series).

> To Adam and Eve in their Eden home,
> nature was full of the knowledge of God,
> teeming with divine instruction.
> To their attentive ears it was vocal with the voice of wisdom.
> Wisdom spoke to the eye and was received into the heart,
> for they communed with God in His created works.
> The book of nature, which spread
> its living lessons before them,
> afforded an exhaustless source of instruction and delight.
> On every leaf of the forest and stone of the mountains,
> in every shining star, in earth and sea and sky,
> God's name was written.
> With both the animate and the inanimate creation—
> with leaf and flower and tree, and with every living creature,
> from the leviathan of the waters to the mote in the sunbeam—
> the dwellers in Eden held converse,
> gathering from each the secrets of its life.
> God's glory in the heavens, the innumerable worlds in their
> orderly revolutions, "the balancings of the clouds" (Job 37:16),
> the mysteries of light and sound, of day and night—
> all were objects of study by the pupils of earth's first school.
> (Ellen G. White, *Child Guidance*, pp. 45, 46)

Chapter 11

Due North

As the needle to the pole, a true friend points upward.

> If nobody smiled and nobody cheered
> and nobody helped us along,
> If each every minute looked after himself
> and good things all went to the strong,
> If nobody cared just a little for you,
> and nobody thought about me,
> And we all stood alone in the battle of life,
> what a dreary old world it would be!
> —Edgar A. Guest in "The Making of Friends"

Cheechakos in the Wilderness

"Why in blazes do you choose to live way up in the Canadian wilderness?" friends would ask us when we visited our homeland. "You could have such lucrative jobs down here in the States?" We had to ask ourselves a milder form of that question when we read the ad Jere's mother sent us from an old copy of the *Quiet Hour Echoes* magazine in our first year of marriage advertising a "farm for sale in Canada." We had both considered the positives of living in Canada before we were married, so when Roy, the seller of the 467 acres in British Columbia's Sukunka Valley, accepted our offer by phone, our life goals crystallized. Jere would begin to realize his dream of having a wilderness school—a wish he'd made as a teen-ager when a dedicated teacher spent a weekend with a few boys, chosen for their rebellious spirit.

Jere's wilderness experience continued to magnetize his blood northward, regardless of any number of numerous lucrative microbiology job offers in keeping with his accumulation of university degrees. Instead of living where he could get employment in his area of expertise, Jere knew he had to live, not just in the country, but as close to the heart of nature as he could get. When our land purchase materialized, he considered the acreage in the Sukunka River Valley to be our heritage. For the first year of our relocation, our native Indian friends called us "Cheechakos," a Cree term that, loosely translated, means "greenhorns who might not survive their first year in the north."

Despite the naysayers who claimed that young people would never come to a campus without electricity, our training facility soon had a waiting list. We were always in need of more housing, regardless of how many rough-hewn homes we erected with wood from trees grown in the surrounding forest.

When Jed was born, at exactly the beginning of our third year in northern British Columbia, we encouraged his love of the out-of-doors and tried to help him maintain quietness of soul. As his horizons expanded with his dog, Tramp, he became one with his world.

Nestled serenely in the foothills of the western Rockies with their wildlife, river, and dense forests, he felt at home. When circumstances dictated that we begin an unwanted and, as it turned out, treacherous sojourn to the south, Jed was badly burned. When his respirator was removed and he could speak again, his first words were, "Dad, I want to go back to Canada." Doors opened providentially, and this time we stayed. Now able to return to Canada, we repurchased our beloved acreage that we had named "Sanctuary Ranch." The return to Canada multiplied our appreciation for our northern heritage. (A more complete version of our journey through fire is recorded in *Rainbow in the Flames,* the first book in this series.)

Champion was the most valuable possession we had during our sojourn; he had become Jed's best friend just prior to his burn accident, and he helped him cope with his new identity as a survivor better than either his mother or father were able to do. There were several boys his age in the little town of Chetwynd who, like Trevor, re-opened their hearts to Jed, looked past his scars, and accepted him as if his accident had never happened.

Friend Ben

Ben was not a Canadian. His friendship with Jed was a stateside inheritance; Jere and I knew his parents before we were married, and our paths crossed many times through the years. When we were in their vicinity, the boys celebrated together, for their birthdays are just two weeks apart, although Ben is a couple of years younger than Jed.

It was only natural that Ben would visit Jed's northern world as their friendship matured. The two of them enjoyed many backwoods adventures together, including the day a spruce grouse flew in front of the four-wheeler at handlebar level and ended up in Jed's lap! Amidst violent flapping, feathers flying, and much squawking, hollering and laughing, the undignified but highly enlightened hen was released to her respective dwelling place. She must have passed the knowledge along to her chicks, for the repetition of the "chicken-in-the-lap" dance has never recurred. Jed appreciated Ben's sense of humor and was especially amused when Ben tongue-tangled his words into Spoonerisms.

Ben came up with his folks to visit us not long after we arrived back in British Columbia. In his later teens, he stayed with us for a couple of weeks one winter, bringing his ice skates with him. They had some hilarious adventures on the ice.

Hockey Pucks Don't Float

When John, the owner of the nearby golf course, phoned to let us know that the ice on his little five-acre lake was thick enough for skating, Jed and Ben gobbled their lunch, donned their insulated coveralls, woolen stocking caps, and mitts, seized their skates, and rushed out the door. It was cold enough outside that ice fog formed before they could close the door. At the time, Jere was teaching at Northern Lights College, and I was thankful to be staying indoors with Jed's aging pal, Champion.

The golf course was drifted with more than two feet of snow, but prevailing winds had cleared the ice. Without grooming—not even pushing so much as a shovel full of snow—the lake was ready for an afternoon of adventure.

Wanting to be sure that the ice would support his weight (Ben is taller and heavier than Jed), Ben decided to inspect the test hole in the north end of the lake. The ice looked to be a good ten inches thick, so Ben was ready for action. Grabbing the puck, he headed to the south end of the lake, spun around, dropped the puck, and walloped a slap shot northward.

Jed attempted to intercept the missile at center-ice, but the puck appeared to be travelling at about the speed of sound and didn't begin to slow until just before it entered the cattails at the north end of the lake. Like a finely tuned putt, it slowed and, as if remote-controlled, navigated its way toward the only hole in the lake—John's tiny test hole. Without so much as a splash, it disappeared silently beneath the surface. Ben had slapped a hole-in-one! Now that was something he could write home about! The boys looked at each other in disbelief.

"Ben!" Jed hollered. "We gotta get the puck back!" (It must be that Jed's Scottish ancestry allowed him only one puck per game.)

"How would we *do* that?" Ben asked with a frown. "The *suck* is *punk* ... I mean, the puck is sunk!"

"Well, you wanna play, right?" Jed asked, as they skidded to a stop at the hole and peered down into the dark depths of the lake.

"Well, yeah ... but how ... maybe they oughtta make pucks that float," Ben whined. Then he placed his mittened hand on his chin, tilted his head sideways, grinned his characteristically exaggerated "bright idea" smile, and lifted his pointer finger in front of Jed's face. Then he jammed the handle of his hockey stick down into the hole.

"If it's not too far to the bottom I should be able to … yeah, I can *stoke* it with my *pick* … er … poke it with my stick!"

"No, Ben!" Jed insisted, raising his hand. "Don't press the puck into the mud! I won't be able to *reach* it! It's not too far from shore. I've retrieved hundreds of golf balls from this lake. It's shallow where the cattails grow!"

"You mean you're gonna put your arm down in this *mold cuck* … er, cold muck?" Ben repeated incredulously as Jed pulled down the top half of his insulated coveralls, tore off his flannel shirt, assumed the horizontal, and then plunged his arm into the icy depths beneath the six-inch hole. The water was up to his armpit before he could touch bottom.

"You … you …!" Jed chattered through clenched teeth. "You pressed the puck clear down into the mud! I can touch it, but I can't … quite grab it! Hold onto my skate blades and lower me a little deeper!"

While Ben played anchor, Jed gained just enough slack to retrieve the treasure. Tossing the muddy puck to Ben, he quickly wiped his arm as best he could, put his shirt back on, and pulled up his coveralls. The remainder of the game was played with incidental jostling about the legalities of the length of the court and the width of goals, as outlined by their boots in lieu of goalposts.

While Jed and Ben discussed Ben's unbelievable hole-in-one goal over mugs of hot cocoa at the kitchen table, I laughed till I cried. When I recovered my composure, I was left with a lingering sense of fulfillment that I found difficult to articulate. Jed's childhood request had come true—again. Like Trevor, Ben was another close friend that Jed could laugh with and make happy memories without compromising his integrity.

Lure of Friendship

It was along the banks of our beautiful Sukunka River that Jed first acquired his interest in navigating the northern waters and his leanings toward search and rescue. As summer progressed, the level of his swimming hole, a shallow backwater beside our picnic grounds at the bend in the river, would diminish until it became mere puddles in the sand, trapping miscellaneous life forms. Whenever we had a picnic, Jed would transfer stranded fingerlings and pollywogs to the safety of the main stream. His disinterested act of kindness as a child, re-stocked the river for his catch-and-release fishing adventures in his later years.

Ben enjoyed fishing even more than Jed did. The cold northern waters lured him to explore their mysterious depths, and therein lies the foundation of more stories than can be condensed into a single volume. Twice, in one summer, Ben almost lost his precious "double-aught" spinners. Attempts to recount the incident of the second lure escape still send the two of them into breathless paroxysms of uninhibited glee.

Lost Lure

Jere and Jed have always practiced catch and release with barbless hooks unless the fish happened to be of the aggressive breed of northern pike that was accidentally introduced into our river a few years ago. These pike are a serious threat to all other species. Ben adopted the same philosophy of catch and release (it only makes sense for a vegetarian) and was looking forward to an afternoon on the river.

"A hot day" is a relative term in the North Country. Any temperature over 75 degrees Fahrenheit (23 Celsius) on a cloudless day qualifies as "hot." The boys often had lively discussions about the pros and cons of Canadian versus U. S. methods of measurement. (Ben had only recently learned what a Robertson screw head looks like. Canadian P. L. Robertson turned down Henry Ford's request to license and remanufacture the screw with the square impression in the head. It is now the most frequently used screw in Canada, especially in boat building.) While they worked on splitting wood, refilling the indoor wood boxes and hoeing the garden, they spent that "hot" July morning combining their country chores with the planning of their favorite afternoon activity—fishing.

By lunchtime, the boys had no inclination to resist the lure of the Sukunka, a meandering body of clear green water running for more than a mile along the western border of our land. By late November, the ice on the Sukunka is often at least a foot thick, a safe and scenic setting in which to skate. With break-up (a classic northern phenomenon) in the springtime, the Sukunka becomes a roaring torrent (from which I once had rescued Champion by his collar). Though it never does warm up much, I know of no more perfectly peaceful place than the beautiful Sukunka in the summertime. Although Champ loved going to the river, he opted to keep his aging body at home that mid-summer day and wholeheartedly endorse Jed and Ben's friendship.

It was back in the days before Ben had graduated to a proper tackle box; he kept his lures in pill bottles that his father had donated to the cause. A pill bottle was portable, fitting nicely into his back pocket. That summer, Ben was hooked on the effectiveness of the double-aught spinner. His motley collection of lures from home included two of these sparkling little rarities marked with "00" (rare because, according to Ben, our northern shops were ill-supplied with that particular jewel). Having lost one of the precious aughts earlier in the week, Ben could not afford to lose his last one; the going rate for teen employment was a mere five dollars an hour, and many tempting lures classified themselves right out of a Ben's budget.

Dressed in their long swim shorts and tee shirts, the boys waded barefoot into the warmer edge water near the riverbank. Ben quickly landed, and released, a couple of graylings with his favorite little double-aught spinner. Then he reached into the pocket of his swim trunks, pulled out his pill bottle and exchanged his little double-aught for a colorful articulating spoon, hoping to land the more exciting fighter, a northern pike. Jed helped Ben reinforce his line with a metal lead against the shark-like razor sharp layers of pike teeth that will sever any other fishing line.

When their legs numbed from the cold as they waded deeper into the northern waters, the boys decided to thaw out on a sandy stretch of shoreline. When they were sufficiently warmed, they put on their dry clothes and hiked alongshore to see what they could discover. They found a beaver house, watched some shorebirds, swatted mosquitoes among the willows, and then headed back to Riverbend—our usual picnic site. That's when Ben patted his back pocket to reassure himself that his "00" treasure was safe. He came up empty-handed! His precious pill bottle was gone!

"Jed!" he croaked. "My lures! They're gone!"

"What?" Jed shook his head in unbelief. "When did you last have them?"

"Uh ... I dunno ... a half hour ago ... when I *dot gressed* ... uh, got dressed, I think."

"That was a *long* time ago, Ben!" Jed frowned, clucking his tongue against the side of his cheek—his characteristic way of indicating a hopeless situation. "There's not much chance of retrieving them now if they're in the river." They walked in silence until they broke out of the underbrush where Ben began a feverish search at the edge of the willows.

> *"Jed!" he croaked. "My lures! They're gone!"*

"Hey, Ben!" Jed shouted, looking farther downstream. "I think I see them! Isn't that your pill bottle bobbing in the middle of the river just upstream from the tramway?" (Jed was referring to a cable car that runs from our side of the river to the opposite shore so that the government survey crews can record the water levels at different seasons near where the High Hat River empties into the Sukunka. From there the Sukunka waters join the Pine, then the Murray, the Peace, and the Athabasca in the Arctic.) Ben strained his eyes northward.

"It *is!*" shouted Ben. Tossing aside his pole and kicking off his boots, he ran alongshore, intermittently hopping on one foot while he pulled off each sock, one at a time, in order to maintain a semblance of momentum, keeping an eye on his treasure bobbing far out in the middle of the river.

"Hurry, Ben!" Jed was laughing so hard that he could hardly keep his balance as the comedy unfolded. "If you don't reach those lures, they'll end up in the Athabasca."

Sock-free at last, Ben began shedding his clothes and his modesty, in a colorful trail that would insure one layer of dry clothing for the chilly evening ride home. With only one piece of clothing remaining to preserve decency, Ben quickly splashed through the shore water and took the plunge.

"Yowie!" he hollered, as he galloped toward midstream at a full speed and began propelling himself forward with his long arms—not unlike a sternwheeler flailing in rapid circles—and was soon nearly up to his neck. "It's C-C-COLD!" he stuttered.

In the end, Ben did recover his prize lures, including his precious double-aught. His moment of victory appeared to render him impervious to the frigid water, but he quickly made his way to a sandy beach, stood for a while in the sunshine, as he reveled in the warmth of triumph. Then he travelled slowly back toward Jed, clothing himself as he walked back up the river.

Jed was still laughing when Ben returned. He laughed all the way home and laughed while he told me the story. He still laughs whenever he pictures Ben's rescue mission, sometimes saying he wished he had a picture of Ben's downstream run. Ben, who is now an excellent photographer, is aware that the best pictures are not captured on film, or even highly digitalized photos; they are the precious, indelible memories that are carried in the heart.

Traveling Homeward

I was privileged to listen in on a meaningful conversation when I happened to be with Jed and Ben on a trip. The three of us had stopped by a home where two youngsters, in flaunting their lack of parental control, left me physically injured. We finished our business as soon as possible and were soon on the road again. It was Ben's voice that finally broke the uncharacteristic silence.

"I've seen some undisciplined children," said Ben, "but these are the *curst wase*, uh ... worst case ever! How do children get out of control like that?"

"Maybe children are born wild," Jed commented, "and it's a parent's job to tame them."

"Makes ya wanna *twink thice*."

I lay on the back seat, still hurting but eager to hear the outcome of this conversation. There was a long silence following Jed's observation, during which I considered my own lack of consistency in the discipline department. I was grateful for the evidence that Jere's sterner virtues overruled my weakness.

> The characters formed in this life
> will determine the future destiny....
> Parents should neglect no duty on
> their part to benefit their children.
> They should so train them that
> they may be a blessing to society here
> and may reap the reward of eternal life hereafter.
> (Ellen G. White, *Child Guidance*, pp. 229, 230)

"I wonder," Jed continued, "if not in childhood, how and when does a person learn to control his emotions? You and I might complain to each other that our parents have been too strict, but today's demonstration puts things in clear perspective."

Ben agreed.

One day, Jed would probably face the challenge of where to raise his children, but more importantly would be his decision about *how* he would raise them—hopefully facing "due north."

> The greatest want of the world is the want of men—
> men who will not be bought or sold,
> men who in their inmost souls are true and honest,
> men who do not fear to call sin by its right name,
> men whose conscience is as true to duty
> as the needle to the pole,
> men who will stand for the right though the heavens fall.
> (Ellen G. White, *Education*, p. 57)

What is manhood, boasted much?
Something we can sense or touch?
Can it be a brilliant thing
Like a jewel in a ring?
Can the teller in a bank
Add it up and place its rank?
Can surveyors draw a line
Separating yours from mine,
Marking with their rigid arts
Where it ends and where it starts?

What is manhood? How and when
Comes this treasured thing to men?
When depleted is the store,
Can a rich man order more,
Or a poor man from his lot
Sell to him who has it not?
Can you save it, would you say,
For the far-off rainy day,
Spurning many a simple need
For one great and glorious deed?

What is manhood? Tell us, sage!
Printed letters on a page?
Victory wreaths or medals bright?
Any cornered beast will fight,
Any man who's trouble free
Very fair will seem to be.
So, I fancy, deeper lies
This rare gift which mortals prize:
'Tis the thought and not the deed,
'Tis the spirit, not the creed.

What is manhood, boasted much?
Nothing we can hold or touch.
'Tis for truth to battle on
When the last false friend is gone;
It is living, conscience clear,
Day by day and year by year,
Suffering loss and taking gain,
Letting neither leave a stain;
Being warrior, neighbor, friend,
Brave and patient to the end.
—Edgar A. Guest, "Manhood"

Sanctuary Lake, as seen from the porch of Jere and Jed's wilderness cabin. Jed and Ben enter the reflection of Mount Wapiti in our faithful old canoe, *The Singing Loon*, early one memorable summer morning.

Chapter 12

All Growed Up

*Gentleman's farewell; the crowning
act of a true champion.*

> I wonder how the roses there
> Will get along without his care,
> An' how the lilac bush will face
> The loneliness about the place;
> For ev'ry spring an' summer he
> Has been the chum o' plant an' tree,
> An' ev'ry livin' thing has known
> A comradeship that's finer grown,
> By havin' him from year to year.
> Now very soon they'll all be here,
> An' I am wonderin' what they'll say
> When they find out he's marched away.
> —Edgar A. Guest in "The Lonely Garden"

When nothing else will melt a human heart, God speaks to His abused and hurting children in the language of animals. Imagine what it must have been like for Adam and Eve in their perfect world, fresh from the hand of their Creator! What joy to experience a world of animals without fear. Every once in a while, someone who is fearful, someone who has never cared to become acquainted with animals, will stumble across one particular creature who steals his or her heart. It may be an injured bird, an abused or neglected dog, or an emaciated kitten that shows up on the doorstep. These seeming coincidences very often coincide with a "dark valley incident" in the life of the benefactor. Unlimited are the number of first-person accounts of incidents in which the rescuer was rescued by his pet, either physically or emotionally. Never entertain a doubt that these are divine appointments. The fact that pets rarely outlive us leaves us homesick for heaven.

According to one Bible prophet, there will be an animal school in the new earth, an ongoing education to better acquaint us with our beloved Creator. Watching His children play with animals is a scene that will bring joy to the Father's parental heart. Isaiah's description begs to be set to music, a happy children's melody, such as a variation on "It's a Small World."

> The wolf also shall dwell with the lamb,
> and the leopard shall lie down with the kid;
> and the calf and the young lion and the fatling together;
> and a little child shall lead them.
> And the cow and the bear shall feed;
> their young ones shall lie down together:
> and the lion shall eat straw like the ox....
> They shall not hurt nor destroy in all my holy mountain:
> for the earth shall be full of the knowledge of the LORD,
> as the waters cover the sea.
> (Isaiah 11:6, 7, 9)

Losing one of these soft, warm friends leaves a very real wound in the heart of their benefactor. Though the story may not all be true, Wilson Rawls captures this depth of loss in his book, *Where the Red Fern Grows*, in which the main character narrates in first person. Young Billy describes losing his pair of Redbone Coonhounds, Old Dan and Little Ann, and he can't eat or sleep. Deeply concerned that their grieving son might mourn to his death, Billy's parents try to encourage him.

"Billy, there are times in a boy's life when he has to stand up like a man. This is one of those times. I know what you're going through and how it hurts, but there's always an answer. The Good Lord has a reason for everything He does."

"There couldn't be any reason for my dogs to die, Papa," I said. "There just couldn't. They hadn't done anything wrong.... If He gave them to me, why did He take them away?"

My father was a firm believer in fate. To him everything that happened was the will of God, and in His Bible, he could always find the answers. Papa could see that his talk had very little effect on me....

Some time in the night I got up, tiptoed to my window, and looked out at my doghouse. It looked so lonely and empty sitting there in the moonlight.... I didn't know I was crying until I felt the tears roll down my cheeks.

Mama must have heard me get up. She came in and put her arms around me. "Billy," she said, in a quavering voice, "You'll just have to stop this. You're going to make yourself sick and I don't think I can stand any more of it."

"I can't, Mama," I said. "It hurts so much, I just can't. ... Mama, do you think God made a heaven for all good dogs?"

"Yes," she said. "I'm sure He did. ... From what I've read in the Good Book, Billy, He put far more things up there than we have here. ... Do you feel better, now?"

"It still hurts, Mama" I said, as I buried my face in her dress, "but I feel a little better."

"I'm glad," she said, as she patted my head. "I don't like to see my little boy hurt like this."

Whether dogs have an actual heaven beyond the one we create for them here is not for me to confirm or deny. It is, however, not difficult for me to believe that the same Jesus who walked this earth for thirty-three short years, turned water into wine, multiplied the bread, healed the sick, and raised the dead, could also return a beloved pet to our arms. He would never have made animals if He didn't love them, and, according to the prophet Isaiah, the new earth is where we will continue, through ceaseless ages, to learn about His love. Perhaps He has provided our bond with animals as the beginning of that eternal existence even now.

Isaiah paints such a delightful scene of animals and children playing together in the new earth that I can easily picture myself meeting up with pets who have helped me trust the God of the clouds to supply the rainbows. Champ was able to pass the lesson of trust and joy on to Jed. Together, we were always watching for rainbows.

Always the Gentleman

Would that every child could grow up with a Champion, a friend such as our beloved dog proved to be. Champ was never happier than when he was with Jed. Jed didn't have to perform any special feats of heroism; his presence was adequate. What fun they had!

In spite of how much he loved him, Champion disappointed Jed in two ways: he wouldn't chase cats and he wouldn't play fetch. A cat had been the object of distraction we had used in training him off leash, so I explained to Jed that I thought Champ had sacrificed the normal pleasure a dog enjoys in chasing cats in favor of obedience, and that playing fetch appeared to be beneath his dignity.

"Champion is not an actor, or a show-off, Jed," I told him. "He's a gentleman."

But one hot day on the bank of the mighty Fraser River in south central British Columbia, Champion condescended to prove his doggie skills. The memory never fails to bring me a smile. Not far from where we were eating our picnic lunch, a huge pit bull was diving from a large rock into the tumultuous river, repeatedly returning a large stick to his master. Champion, after sniffing along the sand enough that he felt it was a safe place for us, settled down beside me in the shade. Jed threw a stick for

Champ to bring back to him, but, as always, Champ would have none of it. Jed couldn't help voicing his disappointment.

"Mom, why won't Champion fetch like Kujo?"

"I don't know Jed," I said, digging my hands down into the cool sand, "I guess no one ever taught him. It's just not in his blood." Champion, lying with one paw over the other, head erect, and eyes closed, appeared aloof and regal. "He's more the mannerly type."

I laid down in the sand, closed my eyes, and listened to the roar of the river as it rushed through the steep-walled canyon. I smiled, thankful that I didn't have to worry about Jed and Champ playing in that dangerous river. Just as I was drifting off to sleep, I felt a thud on my chest. Opening my eyes, I saw Champion standing over me. When he saw that I was awake, he wagged his tail and woofed. On my chest was a stick of driftwood—just the size and shape that someone might choose to throw if a dog wanted to play fetch. Holding Champ's stick in my hand, I sat up. Champ looked at me, then at the stick. His eyes followed the stick and his tail wagged when I moved it. I could not ignore his change in behavior—he wanted to play fetch!

> *"Champions" prove their point without losing their dignity, never stooping to grovel.*

Jed was watching as I tossed the stick a short way down the beach. Champion played three perfect rounds of fetch, carefully dropping the stick back into my lap each time. When he was satisfied that we were aware of his skill and could be trusted to keep his secret, he laid back down beside me and resumed his regal position—head erect, one paw over the other. He never "lowered" himself to fetch again. His majestic head, outlined above me that day against the brilliant blue Canadian sky, is a picture that does not appear in any album, but it is an image I hold close to my heart.

"Champions" prove their point without losing their dignity, never stooping to grovel, never stooping to grovel, never subscribing to the senseless repetition of obsessive-compulsive behavior, but always playing the game on their own terms, though always according to the rules of fair play.

"All Growed Up"

"Dear Jesus," my little boy had prayed when Champion was so badly wounded, "Please don't let Champy die till I'm all growed up!"

Throughout Jed's childhood, that same prayer was repeated during times of crisis, especially on the mornings he had to leave Champion for another medical trip to Vancouver.

Except for a patch of white on his muzzle, Champion still appeared young at fifteen years of age. He never had trouble with his hips or legs, a common weakness in German shepherds. However, one cold winter day I noticed that he was walking slower than usual and that his stomach seemed swollen. He'd been eating less and was sometimes vomiting. I feared the verdict even before the vet explained the x-rays.

But always playing the game on their own terms, though always according to the rules of fair play.

"Sorry, Linda," he said, "I'm afraid it's an inoperable tumor. Take Champ home and make him as comfortable as you can. Maybe these diuretic pills will help decrease the swelling." I hid the pills in bits of canned dog food for a couple of doses, but Champion, wise dog that he was, soon associated the "treats" with unquenchable thirst. He required more and more rest and less and less food. His favorite pastime was aromatherapy; on laundry days he would stretch out on the clothes I had sorted to be washed, burying his sensitive nose in the comforting odors of those he loved best.

As the year-end approached, temperatures reached minus 40 degrees. (Whichever scale you use, it is the same—minus 40° is extremely cold!) Champion spent most of his time indoors snuggled up next to the wood stove. When I addressed our new year's letters, he stretched out beside me. I tried not to look into those trusting amber eyes, knowing that the day was approaching when we would have to face life without him.

For a little extra income, I painted winter scenes on the downtown business windows in Chetwynd, but the traditional holiday cheer eluded me. Jere was on holiday leave, so he stayed with Jed and Champ. Champion always arose from his place beside the stove to greet me like the gentleman he'd always been, but he seemed weaker each evening. I found myself staring at him as he slept.

Curled up in the corner of the couch, I rocked and wept, seeking relief for the ache of the coming void. At these times, Champion would come over and lay on the floor beside the couch near enough that I could rest my hand on his noble head.

"Good boy, Champion," I would assure him. I told him what a wonderful dog he was and how he had been Jed's best friend in every sense of the word. How could I ever find the courage to say the words that would end the life of such a wonderful friend?

Champion hung his head in shame when he deposited an undigested meal beside the door. As those incidents became more common, Champ became steadily weaker. The day came when he was unable to climb the stairs to Jed's bedroom to waken him as usual.

We hung Champ's stocking and filled it with treats, hoping not to face the crisis until after the New Year, but it was not to be. On the morning of December 11, 1995, Jere came to me much too soon with the verdict I so dreaded.

"It's time, Linda," he said quietly. I wanted to close my ears, to run and hide. Instead, I picked up my purse and gave our beloved Champion one last command. "Champ, heel."

Slowly, he took his position beside me, on my left, obedient as always. When he reached the car, he was too weak to climb into the front passenger seat where he so loved to ride co-pilot. Feeling like a traitor to his trust, I helped him into the car. That day he did not play co-pilot. Our Champion lay with his head in my lap as I slowly drove the much-too-short distance to the veterinarian clinic.

Deluged by Precious Memories

I relived the night of his adoption—how had Champ known that his own family could not keep him? How had he known that he must persuade me to go home with him that last night in Brush Prairie? How had he, a mere rookie, proved to be the best among all the dogs in obedience class? Why had his blue ribbon not burned when the cabin caught fire? How had I found him in the old schoolhouse when he was too weak to come home?

The pictures I had stored in my heart clicked softly in my memory: Champ's choice to become part of our family, his ability to make me understand his thought process, our first trip together, his traveling skills, his wisdom, his joyful obedience, his blue ribbon, his pressing his nose against Jed's hospital window, his protecting Jed from bears and hunting rats, and his picking berries (yes, Champ picked raspberries and strawberries, but didn't care for saskatoons or cranberries).

Champ had led the way on Jed's first steps toward healing, away from the flames, up the long and difficult path to the ranger station when Jed was so badly burned. Did an angel tell him, the day before we moved to California, that he'd be needed to help heal the scars on his master's heart, to help him learn how shadows point to rainbows, to prepare him to accept the love of his life? Like the desert rainbow that miraculously appeared before me without rain or sunshine when I felt so lost and alone, Champion convinced me, many times, that God was watching over us. He was a promise wrapped in fur. He had never forsaken us.

From the beginning to the end of every trail, Champion had been there for us. This trail was not leading where I wanted it to go. I laid my hand on Champion's soft head, a prayer of grateful agony escaping my lips.

Lord, thank You so much for giving us Champion. This precious gift has reassured us that You are a God of love. Please help us through this valley. It hurts so much to lose our Champion. We will miss him so much. I've always pictured Cookie and Tramp waiting on the front porch of my mansion. Would You please let Champ be there, too, if possible? He has helped us find rainbows, even in the dark. Comfort us in this great loss. Amen.

I rubbed Champ's ear, the way he liked—way down inside. He groaned in rapture. I ran my fingers through his fur. His head was moist with my tears.

End of the Trail

Jed had gone to town for truck parts earlier in the day. I'd left a message at NAPA to have him to meet me at the vet's office. Shortly after I arrived, Jed came into the lobby and knelt beside his Champion.

Jed is seventeen, nearing six feet tall, but he will never outgrow his gratitude to Champ's faithfulness. Is it ever the right time to say goodbye? Hearts that have suffered together need no words. I couldn't talk—even if I tried. A hard lump lodges tightly in my throat. As the vet calls my name, my weak legs do not want to walk.

"I'll hold him, Mom," Jed says, quietly scooping Champion up in his strong arms, bearing the burden that I cannot. Jed walks to the exam room and gently lays Champ on the stainless-steel table. Champion has always submitted willingly to injections, but the vet has to wrestle against his resistance this time. Even in his weakened condition Champ seems to know, and he is not prepared to lay aside his assignment of a lifetime. Champion is a gentleman, but he has no intention of slipping quietly into the night. With his last feeble efforts, he resists leaving his beloved boy.

Why can't this unthinkable decision be followed by a quiet, uncomplicated, peaceful ceremony? Why must we face such terrible agony, Lord? My boy has had enough pain to last a lifetime.

"Jed, hold Champ firmly, please," the doctor says without emotion.

Jed envelops his devoted friend in a final embrace, burying his face in Champ's glossy coat. When the tetany of death silences the great heart, Jed remains bowed over the quiet form of his beloved friend.

The pale-yellow winter light filtering through the window beside Jed, diffused through my own tears, causes a surreal glow to reflect from the stainless-steel table and shimmer around my son with unearthly luminescence. I experience an intensity of feelings that surpass the emotional upheavals I felt that night, ten short years ago, when Champion came into our lives—the intense mixture of light and shadow that left no room for doubting that God was in control.

A little boy's prayer bursts into flame from somewhere deep in my soul where it has smoldered since the day he prayed it.

"Please, dear Jesus, don't take Champy away till I'm all growed up!"

In that potent heart-wrenching moment my son bids farewell to his childhood. The room spins. Jed walks toward me, tears making crooked trails across his wounded cheeks. I want to scoop my child into my arms and kiss away his pain. Instead, I lean on him. Together, we walk through the door to a future without our Champion.

My little Jedidiah is "all growed up." Would that all might know His call and respond to it as did Jed's beloved Champion. The hole he left with his passing was much larger than the injury he helped to heal in Jed's heart. But that hole had been altered into a chamber just the size and shape that Jed's beloved Amber would one day be able to fill. The carving, smoothing, repairing, and infilling of the emotional and spiritual chambers of the human heart is fine work. Our deepest wounds leave a hole that we can open to the touch of the Master's hand. Healing hearts is the work of God, and there is no wound He cannot heal.

> He healeth the broken in heart,
> and bindeth up their wounds.
> (Psalm 147:3)

If I allow my imagination to think about future possibilities, I can easily picture a gentle German shepherd on the veranda of a certain mansion. The details of the house are unclear, but the dog's features are unmistakable. Without conscious thought, a command rises to my throat.

"Champ, come."

He'll remember. We practiced together so many times.

> Does Jesus care when I've said good-bye
> To the dearest on earth to me,
> And my sad heart aches till it nearly breaks—
> Is it aught to Him? does He care?
>
> O yes, He cares—
> I know He cares!
> His heart is touched with my grief;
> When the days are weary,
> the long nights dreary,
> I know my Savior cares.
> —Frank E. Graeff, "Does Jesus Care?"

Chapter 13

Encircled

"O that everyone might be this happy!"
—Jed Franklin, 2017

The Father's presence encircled Christ,
and nothing befell Him but that which infinite love permitted
for the blessing of the world.
(Ellen G. White, *Thoughts from the Mount of Blessing*, p. 71)

Call to Joy

Just as surely as the oak is in the acorn, so are rainbows of joy delicately encased with divine craftsmanship into every drop of rain that falls on humankind. With the shattered pieces of our broken dreams, God reshapes, with our permission, a purpose and mission not included in our original design for happiness. It is beyond human ability to reason out the blueprint for happiness—ours or anyone else's. True joy comes in understanding our purpose. It comes in truthfully answering the three paramount questions that come with the gift of life— (1) who am I? (2) where do I come from?

> *Fortunately, a "seeing-heart dog" helped Jed surmount the early stumbling blocks of grief and disappointment.*

and (3) where am I going? Jed considered these questions very carefully—especially during his teen years.

Fortunately, a "seeing-heart dog" that helped Jed surmount the early stumbling blocks of grief and disappointment that could have immobilized him after he acquired his burn injury and helped him recognize the value of a certain young lady who brought, in her train, immeasurable bliss.

God's Plan

Before Jed turned five, I began praying that the Lord would create a woman fit for his specific needs. I had no picture in my mind regarding the specifics of the finished product, nor when the miracle might happen. Yet, I was sure that, in God's time, the dream would come true. Jed was not so sure—especially after the burn accident.

"Mom, who will love me now?" he questioned. "I'm all scarred up."

"She will be coming here," I assured him from a warm place in my heart well cultivated by an oft-repeated impression. "Grow your character to be the person you want her to be."

Like Isaac's Rebekah, when Jed was found doing the work he was called to do, Amber was brought to him from a far country—in the fullness of time. No search on Jed's part could have come up with such an exact model as the young lady I love as the mother of my grandchildren.

Happy as he is in his role as husband and father, Jed's heart was uncertain that he should even hope that this type of joy could actually come to pass. I'm convinced that the trustworthiness and unconditional acceptance of his faithful dog, Champion, helped Jed grow his injured boy-heart into a trusting man-heart. His faith, strong in so many other ways, was weakened by his damaged appearance, no matter how I tried to assure him that the one God would choose as his helpmate would be looking much deeper than mere face value.

> Oh, for living, active, faith!
> We need it; we must have it,
> or we shall faint and fail in the day of trial.
> The darkness that will then rest upon
> our path must not discourage us,
> or drive us to despair.
> It is the veil with which God covers
> His glory when He comes to impart rich blessings.
> (Ellen G. White, *Christian Experience and Teachings*, p. 190)

Heart Transformation

When the explosion came that rocked my little boy's world, leaving him scarred and disoriented, Champion was right beside him, patiently waiting for him to heal, encouraging him not to close his heart to joy. This intelligent animal conducted his boy into manhood—through the clouded world of pain and the shadowy veil of disfigurement that could have robbed Jed of the completeness with which God had planned to bless him. Champion lifted those little injured hands, limp with doubt, impotent to grasp life's full potential, and strengthened them with practical exercise.

When love was offered him by a petite and talented young woman from Montana—that pure, perceptive, and loyal love that Jed had hardly dared hope for—his heart had been, in large part, pried open by the love and trust of his Champion. Jed and Amber were both praying for, and open to, divine guidance. They had practiced laying their will on God's side—long before they met each other. Their beautifully constrained love story and their choice of using His protective method of courtship were a witness to their family and friends (see *Rainbow in the Flames,* chapter 20).

As Jed and Amber's wedding day approached, Amber said to him, "I'm so excited! This is a dream come true! I can't imagine what you've been going through this past year!" (This had included the concise requirements of courtship, the claiming of promises, the careful interpretation of providential indicators, and then the patience required to wait for answers from parents before revealing his intents to her.)

"I'm so glad I'm a girl!" she exclaimed.

"Me too!" Jed affirmed with a wink. "Me too."

> All our sufferings and sorrows, all our temptations and trials,
> all our sadness and griefs, all our persecutions and privations,
> in short, all things work together for our good.
> All experiences and circumstances are God's workmen
> whereby good is brought to us.
> (Ellen G. White, *The Ministry of Healing*, p. 488)

With the birth of each child, Jed and Amber continue to seek God's will in raising them to know the joy of surrender as they have experienced it. They both have an uncanny ability to see blessings in the clouds of life from having learned the joy of quiet trust in His timing for all things.

How can joy be the result of such pain and heartache? It's the same for Jed as for any other survivor. Jed revealed the secret not long ago in a statement he made as we watched his young family playing tag on the lawn. "Happiness comes from God; the nearer you get to Him, the more joy you have."

Though they may not recognize it, my grandchildren are the beneficiaries of Champion's lessons, with classes in perseverance, trust, and unconditional love. Where Jed was able to achieve a quiet spirit in the face of adversity, I'm still learning about tough love. In spite of my experience with well-disciplined nurses (who, among other difficult lessons, required me to turn a blind eye to Jed's ineffective efforts to feed himself with his freshly-grafted hands), I nearly fumbled the tutorial ball when my first grandchild unexpectedly tossed an injury she suffered in my direction. My newly formed grandmother arms craved to gather the tearful waif into my arms and kiss away her pain. Barely in time, my heart listened to my head.

"Gettin' Bettah"

I stood expectantly at the foot of her slide while my first grandchild, Hannah, not much more than a year old, with an air of assurance, ascended the ladder. As she climbed, I heard a tender "thunk" and saw her feet pause on the ladder. I heard her quickly inhale a couple of times and then continue climbing. As she crested the top and readied herself to obtain the thrill she'd worked so hard to enjoy, I saw a dab of fresh blood on her mouth.

"Hannah, did you hurt your lip?" I asked. She puffed out her cheeks as if testing her lip for damage and blew her breath out between pursed lips. She sniffed, drew an arm across one leaky eye and repeated the mantra she'd adopted earlier that week, while listening to her mother's prognosis of the blister she'd acquired from her new rubber boots.

"S'gettin' bettah, Gwamma," said the throbbing rosebud mouth, "s'gettin' bettah."

"It's getting better!" What a lesson for Grandma! No noisy indulgence of pain or anger. Not a needy sob. Not even a "Yes, I'm hurting badly now, but it will pass." At the bottom of the slide I held her hand. My heart grasped the value of those early lessons Jed learned in the hospital and then repeated with Champion. That day I re-learned, from the mouth of a mere babe, the lesson I should have permanently adopted as my motto long ago. Yes, tears are a natural reaction to pain, but needless over-indulgence blinds a youngster to the joy of overcoming—a peacefulness of mind that looks beyond discomfort. This strength of spirit, born in adversity, survives the tests of time.

> *As she climbed, I heard a tender "thunk" and saw her feet pause on the ladder.*

A Spoonful of Story

Bumps, bruises, and even blood must not be allowed to spoil our journey. Dwelling in painful shadows can blind us to the light. Stepping out of the darkness puts us in a place where we are available to those who might need to lean on us for encouragement. Pain when overcome is a key in the hand of faith that can open the heart of a fallen fellow traveler. When others look to me for strength, knowing that I have endured a painful trial, I cannot afford to guide them toward a slippery steppingstone of sentimentalism. Offering them a firm hand, gloved in self-discipline, will place them on solid ground.

What better way to help a child see worthwhile life lessons than by true-life stories of triumph? That's where grandparents shine! Their grandchild will say, "Tell me about the time the horse kicked you!" What are they really saying? Are they not inferring a much deeper query involving the faith they might've heard you talk about? "Grandma, please help me understand how God protected you." It's my firm belief that they are baring their little souls for us to plant a seed of faith with the assurance that, "God will protect you, too!"

At that blessed moment, I hold at my fingertips, wrinkled with the passage of time and pain, a clarifying drop of divine eye salve, a shock absorber for the coming bumps on their road of life. I can affirm to my posterity that the shadows of the past do point toward the homeland, for I have felt God's protection and comfort. Looking back through the years, I can see that He did protect me, and it's in my job description to tell how my "close calls" of the past are proof of His loving protection.

Capture your stories, parents and grandparents! Be ready to plant that little glory seed when your golden moment comes!

> And these words, which I command thee this day,
> shall be in thine heart:
> And thou shalt teach them diligently unto thy children,
> And shalt talk of them when thou sittest in thine house,
> And when thou walkest by the way, and when thou liest down,
> and when thou risest up.
> (Deuteronomy 6:6, 7)

Health is an invaluable blessing. Happiness is so important. But discovering your mission in life and inspiring faith in others are the truest forms of joy.

Enticing Ensamples

The same lessons that are learned practically can and must be reinforced in story form, as in the admonition of the Apostle Paul.

> Now all these things happened unto them for ensamples:
> and they are written for our admonition,
> upon whom the ends of the world are come.
> (1 Corinthians 10:11)

Joseph was the beneficiary of such stories. In his inspiring book, *God Sent a Man*, Carlyle B. Haynes tells us that the stories of Joseph's forefathers were enough to inspire him to remain true to the God of his fathers. No doubt Joseph had said to his father and grandfather many times, just as my grandchildren say to me, "Tell me a story ... tell it again."

Joseph learned from the lips of those he trusted that all things, both the good and bad, were planned by the all-powerful God of the universe who was also planning Joseph's life for him with that same great love. Haynes challenged his readers to achieve, in the midst of a life of blatant injustices, to hold to Joseph's level of contentment and peaceful trust.

> If you once believe that a good and all-powerful God has shaped a plan for your life, and is quite able to carry it out for you if you rely on Him under all circumstances, letting nothing shake your conviction in His superintending providence for you, then your whole outlook on life, current events, and your environment will be so changed as to bring you the most satisfying and abundant

> life anyone can ever have. You can have *a life in which nothing goes wrong* and in which all the disciplines of life are allowed to mold you into the person that God wants you to be, made after His own image in complete harmony with His all-ruling will. (Carlyle B. Haynes, *God Sent a Man*, foreword, emphasis supplied)

The essence of Joseph's experience and his attitude toward everything that happened to him can be encapsulated in a single verse, Genesis 50:20, in which he addresses the eleven brothers who sold him into slavery.

To put it as we would say it today, Joseph said, "It's OK! I forgive you! Although you meant to harm me, God has used it for good so that many people can be saved."

Will I one day look back over my life and be able to accept the fact that, like Joseph, I would choose to be led the exact way He has led me, including the clouds and shadows I so very much resented? Hear Joseph's resounding, "Yes!" ringing down the corridors of time.

> God never leads His children otherwise
> than they would choose to be led,
> if they could see the end from the beginning,
> and discern the glory of the purpose
> which they are fulfilling as co-workers with Him.
> (Ellen G. White, *The Desire of Ages*, pp. 224, 225)

Oh, that my eyes, like those of Joseph and of Jesus, might be opened to the glorious possibilities of being encircled like a rainbow by the knowledge of God's presence, regardless of weather conditions.

Chapter 14

Living Under the Rainbow

Sharing Survival Skills.

When Life Seems Unfair

In 2011, Jed was asked by the British Columbia Professional Firefighters to write an essay to post on "The Future is Mine," an adult Burn Survivor Program directed by Ann Coombs with a variety of social, support, and educational programs. The following is his commentary, a year before his marriage. Its principles seem to apply to more than just burn injuries.

> **Against the Wall**
>
> Have you ever considered what life would be like if you could eliminate the pain of your past? You could be a different person. In my case there would be no burn injury, no hospital stays, and no surgeries or scars. Sounds great! But what would I risk by losing that physical and mental pain?
>
> Let's go back farther to a time in your life when, as a young child, your parents said "No." You felt pain, emotionally. It was for your best good that you were not allowed to play in the street. By disobeying, you may have received a physical correction to remind you about the importance of obedience.
>
> This pain caused a difference in your life, for better or worse, depending on how you responded to the discipline. You may have

been angry and rebellious, or sad and discouraged. Better yet, you could have chosen to learn from your pain and cheerfully gotten on with your life.

In my experience, with the combination of physical and mental pain that a burn injury inflicts, I have had all of these reactions, and have come to hate the first of these responses because that response trapped me in my pain, unable to move forward.

I was eight years old when my life was threatened by gasoline fumes from a generator I was filling with fuel. When the fumes ignited, I was thrown against an interior wall of the small building that housed the generator and was completely engulfed in 1200°F flames. I thought my life was over, but I couldn't just quit and die without doing my best to survive. I said to myself, "Don't panic, Jed!"

I knew that the generator was in front of the door—my only way of escape—but in the heat and flames I dared not open my eyes. Which way was out? I thought that if the generator had exploded, then it would have blown me across the room against the west wall. Since I couldn't see anything, I turned around, took three steps, and jumped. Fortunately, I guessed right, leaped over the generator and through the doorway! By a miracle—and by not giving up—I had discovered the door.

How badly burned was I? Looking down, I saw that I was still on fire, so I rolled on the ground to put it out. Here came Mom. Good, *she* was OK! I was so hot! Mom was trying to get my clothes off, but the plastic zipper of my jacket melted and stuck to her hands. My skin dripped off of my body like hot, white wax.

"Mom, the pond!" I said. She put me in the clean, cold water to cool.

My rescue, first with Mom pushing me uphill for a mile in a wheelbarrow and then by helicopter, is an amazingly miraculous story that Mom has recorded in her first book, *Rainbow in the Flames*. Nearly fifty percent of my body had burns, and most of them were third degree. I freely admit that I had a lot of pain and fear. Thankfully, I was encouraged by my family, medical professionals, and my faithful German shepherd, Champion, to begin a healing journey that included not only my physical healing but that addressed my mental and spiritual needs as well. My concern now is for others who find themselves in need of overcoming the scars that are left by fire.

What to Do with a Burn Injury?
It's amazing how a few seconds of fire can continue to create emotional turmoil if we let it. Physically, the burns may heal fairly well, but the emotional pain can last much longer. A burn injury is a hard experience to learn lessons from, but the alternatives to acceptance and emotional healing are anger, rebellion, sadness, and discouragement. I have learned, like you have, that painful experiences force us to change. My choice is to change for the better, with God's help. I still fight against negative emotions, but less and less.

I believe that I have become a better person through suffering than I would have been without it. My pain has lowered my self-centeredness and pride, which is not something we generally welcome, but it can actually improve our disposition by decreasing selfishness. My happiness is now in helping others: family, God, work, and knowledge.

The Big Question
Not long ago, someone asked me, "If you could, would you change your scars back to normal skin?"

I thought about that. If I could go back twenty-four years [over thirty years and counting, now] to that Friday afternoon and put out that pilot light on the hot water heater that was housed near the generator and started my painful journey with such a blast of force, should I do it? Would I dare? What would I be like without having suffered a burn injury? Is there a possibility that I would be self-centered and unhappy, though probably better looking?

How would you answer that challenge? If you were allowed to do anything that your selfish heart wanted, with no corrections from your parents, nor self-discipline from difficult experiences, would you be a better person today? I have had to conclude that it is in learning from pain that we grow; we gain a character and stability that draws joy and peace like a magnet and brings out the best in ourselves and in others. If we hold onto our pride and keep the pain of our injury ever before us and others, never knowing how to release the accompanying depression and anger, we will bring out the worst in ourselves and those around us. It's a complex challenge to be an overcomer, but now I am content and happy (well, most of the time)! I choose to learn and grow.

> *I have had to conclude that it is in learning from pain that we grow.*

My advice to those of you who find yourselves against a wall: please don't quit! Go forward! It may mean the difference between life and death. It did for me. (Jed Franklin, February 26, 2011)

World Burn Congress 2007

Twenty years after his burn injury (interlaced with earlier video clips they'd recorded of Jed as a youngster in the video *Healing Inside Too* and as a counselor at Vancouver Firefighter's Burn Camp) Jed was interviewed by Miyoung Lee of CBC TV when our family responded to the invitation of Vancouver Firefighters to attend the 2007 World Burn Congress.

> As a child, he survived a horrendous fire, suffered severe burns, but that didn't stop Jed Franklin. Now, twenty years later, he's enjoying a life he never thought he'd have. To many, this is the face of hope. Twenty-nine-year-old Jed Franklin is a burn survivor. He's in Vancouver to be part of the World Burn Congress and to share his story with other survivors.

When he was eight, an accident involving a generator nearly killed him. Doctors wondered if he would survive the year. Jed underwent thirteen surgeries, had his skin scrubbed off and received several skin grafts. When some people would have given up, Jed reached out [to others in Vancouver General Hospital]. His ability to help people didn't stop there [with helping other survivors his age in the VGH burn unit].

For years after, he came to the lower mainland to help other children as a counselor at Burn Camp. Now, at 29, he says he wouldn't trade the experience.

Last fall something that Jed wasn't sure would ever happen ... happened. He got married! Amber Franklin says that when she looks at her husband's face, she doesn't see the scars anymore.

It's these images of Jed, in what he calls his "normal life" that continue to be an inspiration to others.

Joy—the Call to Higher Ground

When Amber's family became part of our country living ministry, Jed allowed himself to consider the possibility that someone might be able to love him for who he was, neither pitying him for his scars nor denying that their existence makes a difference. This recent conversation between Jed and Amber adds credibility to the depth of their relationship.

> **Jed:** When God's sends a gift, *He adds no sorrow with it* (Proverbs 10:22). I'd have to say this is true. I have no regrets marrying you, Amber. It's a blessing that could be too easily taken for granted.
>
> **Amber:** Our marriage is so happy! I love you more now, if possible, than the day I married you! You are my kind, respectful leader.
>
> **Jed:** God has poured us out such a huge blessing that I sometimes feel as if my heart does not have room enough to receive it! I have tried to make the most of what was left after the burn

accident; I am so thankful that everything still works. I have so much more than many people have.

Amber: The joy of having a happy family means more to me than any earthly treasure!

Jed: We still have many faults to overcome and are learning to be content with what we have. I feel that is a real key to happiness—making the most of what we have together is true happiness.

Amber: Our children are our greatest treasure; *"For of such is the kingdom of heaven"* (Matthew 19:14). The children have such simple faith and trust. We must take extra care not to hinder (forbid) them from coming to Jesus; they will be drawn to Him if we do not misrepresent Him. Children are a mirror; I must be consistent with what I require of them and pray earnestly for each one, for they each have battles of their own to fight. Their generation may be tested even more than what we've gone through. I want to be today what I want my children to be tomorrow.

(Jed's story is posted with other burn survivors at https://1ref.us/tj. A video of Jed and Amber's organic grain farm in the Peace Country of northern British Columbia may be viewed at https://1ref.us/tk).

It appears to be Jed's purpose in life to help others discern the beautiful swath of brilliance in the colors that resulted from his own storm. I will attest to the fact that the interaction of the daylight with disaster, deluge, and darkness has been spectacular. God alone sees the picture in its entirety, but it is in the storm that he prepares our eyes for enduring splendor.

> To all who are reaching out to feel the guiding hand of God,
> the moment of greatest discouragement
> is the time when divine help is nearest.
> They will look back with thankfulness
> on the darkest part of their way.
> From every temptation and every trial
> they will come forth with finer faith and a richer experience.
> (Ellen G. White, *Signs of the Times*, January 15, 1902)

Healing is a Choice

Just as Champion had to learn to heel, so must humans learn to heal by following a carefully scripted plan of obedience.

If we'd had the choice, Jere and I would have chosen to prevent Jed's accident, his suffering, and his readjustment. However, Jed is of a different opinion.

"If I could choose between erasing my scars, consequently coming into possession of my old heart, I would not choose to do it. In order to secure my present level of joy, I would endure my injury again. I wouldn't change a thing. I need every lesson learned. By it, my purpose was defined. I am forever grateful."

> God never leads His children otherwise than
> they would choose to be led,
> if they could see the end from the beginning and discern the glory
> of the purpose which they are fulfilling as co-workers with Him.
> (Ellen G. White, *The Ministry of Healing*, p. 479)

Gems from Jed

HEALTHY CHOICES

To heal, we must make healthy choices.
Every decision to promote health is a spiritual decision.
If you take a walk every day, you'll have ten extra years to do it!
Agricultural pursuit is the only job we can do where we can benefit from all eight doctors in one day! (The eight doctors are nutrition, exercise, water, sunshine, temperance, air, rest, and trust in divine power.)
The mind becomes imbalanced by escaping to what we love to do if it's not a healthy choice.

ENDURING HARDSHIP

Our limitations must never define who we are;
weep a little, watch a lot, and then get to work.
Like diamonds, those who endure
the most pressure become the most valuable.
When we feel the blow of the hammer,
we know we have been chosen.
Don't be too hard on yourself. Smile.
Nobody's perfect—at least, not yet!
Our destiny is to channel life-giving current to others.
With purity comes honor.

TRUST THAT EVERYTHING WORKS FOR GOOD

If I'd not lost Tramp, I would not have known Champ;
my heart was carved by injury.
Take care not to question God regarding your trials—
only He knows the whole plan.

SELF CONTROL

Strive to be a person who does not panic or
react in any way without thinking.
The ability to reason is more powerful than
the entire sum of your emotions.
You can tell a lot about a person's character by his car.
Seek to become a wise counselor.

Is it important to be right? Redefine the Battle.

Someone cuts into line in front of me.
That irritates me. I am given an opportunity to get even.
I start lining up the qualifications for vengeance—
(1) Was this person's action right or wrong? Wrong.
(2) Await a providential opportunity to deliver my conviction.
(3) Test by the Law and the Prophets ...
well, if you count an eye for an eye ...
(4) What would Jesus do? He would turn the other cheek.

Jesus leaves no room for vengeance or
getting even or keeping score.

I Can Trust

Just because I cannot see it
Doesn't mean the rainbow's gone.
Just because I cannot hear it
Does not mean there is no song.
Just because I cannot smell it
Won't devalue any flower.
Just because I can't see angels
Won't decrease their mighty power.
Just because the clouds hide sunshine
Does not the least diminish light.
God is with me whensoever
I distrust my finite sight!
—L. Franklin

Bibliography

Works of Ellen White

The Adventist Home. Hagerstown, MD: Review and Herald Publishing Association, 1952.

Child Guidance. Hagerstown, MD: Review and Herald Publishing Association, 1952.

Christian Experience and Teachings. Ellen G. White Estate, 2010.

Counsels on Health. Mountain View, CA: Pacific Press Publishing Association, 1923.

The Desire of Ages. Mountain View, CA: Pacific Press Publishing Association, 1898.

Letter 16, 1897.

The Ministry of Healing. Mountain View, CA: Pacific Press Publishing Association, 1905.

My Life Today. Washington, DC: Review and Herald Publishing Association, 1952.

Our Father Cares. Washington, DC: Review and Herald Publishing Association, 1991.

Selected Messages, book 2. Washington, DC: Review and Herald Publishing Association, 1958.

Testimonies for the Church, vol. 4. Mountain View, CA: Pacific Press Publishing Association, 1881.

Testimonies for the Church, vol. 5. Mountain View, CA: Pacific Press Publishing Association, 1889.
Signs of the Times. January 15, 1902.

Books and Magazines

Blanco, Jack. *The Clear Word*. Washington, DC: Review and Herald Publishing Association, 1994.
Guest, Edgar. *When Day Is Done*. Chicago, IL: The Reilly and Lee Co., 1921.
Selden, Frank. In *Songs of Dogs*, edited by Robert Frothingham. Cambridge: Houghton Mifflin Company, The Riverside Press, 1920.
White, James. "What Heavenly Music." In *The Seventh-day Adventist Hymnal*. Washington, DC: Review and Herald Publishing Association, 1985, 1988.
Widdemer, Margaret. *The Old Road to Paradise.* New York, NY: Henry Hold and Co., 1918.
Wintle, Walter. "Thinking." *Unity Magazine.* Unity Tract Society, Unity School of Christianity, 1905.

Websites

SR Organic Farms. One Degree Organics. https://1ref.us/tk. Accessed Jan 2, 2020.
Survivor Stories Burn Fund. https://1ref.us/tj. Accessed Jan 2, 2020.

We invite you to view the complete
selection of titles we publish at:
www.TEACHServices.com

We encourage you to write us
with your thoughts about this,
or any other book we publish at:
info@TEACHServices.com

TEACH Services' titles may be purchased in
bulk quantities for educational, fund-raising,
business, or promotional use.
bulksales@TEACHServices.com

Finally, if you are interested in seeing
your own book in print, please contact us at:
publishing@TEACHServices.com

We are happy to review your manuscript at no charge.

www.ingramcontent.com/pod-product-compliance
Lightning Source LLC
Chambersburg PA
CBHW050812160426
43192CB00010B/1729